The Common Ha

Thomas Turlis, who was hangman of London from 1752 to 1771 (from an old print).

THE COMMON
HANGMAN

English and Scottish Hangmen
Before the Abolition of Public
Executions

James Bland

ZEON BOOKS

A **Zeon** Book

Original edition published in the United Kingdom in 1984
by Ian Henry Publications

Revised and enlarged edition published in 2001 by Zeon Books

A CIP catalogue record for this book is available from the British
Library

ISBN 1-874113-09-2

Printed and bound in the United Kingdom by
Haynes Publishing
Sparkford, Nr Yeovil,
Somerset, BA22 7JJ

Zeon Books

An associate company of

Zardoz Books
Rivington House,
Whitecroft,
Dilton Marsh, Westbury,
Wiltshire, BA13 4DJ

Contents

Acknowledgements

In the first edition of this book I expressed my gratitude to each of the following for providing me with information during the course of my researches: Donald Galbraith, Deputy Keeper, and Miss Margaret Young, Assistant Keeper, both of the Scottish Record Office, Edinburgh (now the National Archives of Scotland); Dr Walter H. Makey, Edinburgh City Archivist; Mr G. A. Dixon, Assistant Archivist of the Central Regional Council Archives Department, Stirling (now the Stirling Council Archives Service); David Lockwood, Curator of the Dumfries Museum; Miss Judith Cripps, Archivist of the City of Aberdeen District Council (now the Aberdeen City Council); Richard Dell, Principal Archivist of the Strathclyde Regional Archives Department, Glasgow (now the Glasgow City Council Archives Department); the staff of the Glasgow Room of the Mitchell Library, Glasgow; Mr W. T. Barnes, Senior Assistant Archivist of the Department of Manuscripts and Records, National Library of Wales, Aberystwyth; Richard E. Huws of the Department of Printed Books, also of the National Library of Wales; Mr A. G. Veysey, Clwyd County Archivist, Hawarden, Deeside; David Bromwich, Local History Librarian of the Somerset Local History Library (now the Somerset Studies Library), Taunton; the staff of the Somerset Record Office, Taunton, particularly Mr R. J. E. Bush; the staff of the North Yorkshire County Library, Reference and Information Library, York (now the York City Library); the staff of the Tyne and Wear County Council Archives Department (now the Tyne and Wear Archives Service), Newcastle-upon-Tyne; J. Keith Bishop, Lancashire County Archivist, Preston, and the staff of the Archives and Local History Department, Dudley Library (now the Archives and Local History Service, Coseley).

I would now like to thank Miss Alison J. Lindsay, West Search Room Supervisor, and Ian Hill, also of the West Search Room, National Archives of Scotland, Miss Marion M. Stewart, Archivist of the Dumfries and Galloway Council Archives, Alison Scott, Archivist, Edinburgh City Archives, Norman Newton of Highland Libraries, Inverness, Kevin Wilbraham, Archivist, of the Ayrshire Archives, Ayr, Mrs S. Bell of Aberdeen Central Library, and the staff of the Carnegie Library, Ayr, for affording me similar help during the preparation of this revised and enlarged edition.

I also wish to thank Andrew Bethune of the Edinburgh Room, Edinburgh Central Library, Winnie Tyrrell of Glasgow Museums, Robert Evans of Llanstephan, Carmarthenshire, and Harry Taylor, the Commissioning Editor of the *Black Country Bugle*, for helping me to find suitable illustrations for this edition.

Finally, I would like to thank Donald Rumbelow for allowing me to reproduce the picture of Thomas Turlis from his own book *The Triple Tree*, published by Harrap Ltd in 1982.

Introduction

This book deals with the lives, characters and working conditions of English and Scottish hangmen over the course of three centuries, beginning in Tudor times and ending in the reign of Queen Victoria. Unlike more recent members of the profession, most of the hangmen concerned were permanent officials of particular towns or cities. Prior to 1868, they carried out executions in public, generally unmasked and often before large crowds.

Their work was not normally confined to hanging: most of them inflicted public whippings too. Some of the earlier ones also had other, more barbaric, types of execution to perform: beheading, hanging, drawing and quartering or burning in cases of treason, pressing to death in cases in which prisoners 'stood mute' on arraignment for felony. These earlier hangmen usually carried out sentences of branding, mutilation and pillorying and the burning of seditious publications as well.

England invariably had many more executions than Scotland, and London usually had many more than any other town in England. During the Tyburn era the London hangman often 'turned off' dozens, if not scores, of offenders in the course of a single year, while the Edinburgh functionary hanged very few and some provincial hangmen, even in England, hanged nobody at all for years on end. It was also in London that most of the executions for treason took place.

Another duty carried out by some of our London hangmen was the tying together of the thumbs of capital offenders with whipcord before sentence was passed on them. Nobody seems to know the significance of this cruel ritual, or how widely it was practised, but it appears to have been performed regularly at the Old Bailey Sessions House for much of the eighteenth century. For part of that time the same procedure was also used as an alternative means of dealing with prisoners who refused to plead.

Our hangmen's circumstances were thus quite varied, with some having a much wider and more brutal role than others. During the period covered by this book, however, their importance as instruments of justice gradually declined until none of them had any duties to carry out other than hangings. And by that time the use of the death penalty had become so restricted that there were comparatively few of them anywhere in Britain.

The hangmen of those days were, of course, not *just* instruments of justice: they were entertainers as well. For public executions generated much public excitement, and many of them took place in a festive atmosphere, with street venders doing a brisk trade among the crowds. At Tyburn, stands were erected to provide seats for anyone willing to pay for them, and these were often full; other

Tyburn on a hanging day (from an engraving by William Hogarth, 1697-1764).

spectators paid to be allowed to watch the proceedings from houses overlooking the scene. Later, in the nineteenth century, special excursion trains were run to provincial towns where executions were due to take place.

Among the crowds who watched him at work, the hangman usually had many admirers. Some of them occasionally bought pieces of his used ropes, especially those which had been used for the hanging of famous or infamous criminals. Sometimes, after a whipping had been inflicted to the crowd's satisfaction, a collection might even be taken on his behalf.

Yet the hangman himself was rarely a respected figure at this time: indeed, he was often widely despised and sometimes shunned or reviled for the repugnant way in which he earned his living. If, as sometimes happened, he behaved improperly at the gallows, or bungled an execution, he might be attacked by the crowd, either there and then or on his way home afterwards. Sometimes he was attacked for just doing his duty in the normal way.

The hangman's low standing made it impossible for some authorities to induce men of good character to serve in such a capacity: as a result, they sometimes had to employ drunkards or even criminals as executioners. In some cases, the hangman was an offender who had accepted the post in order to avoid punishment himself; in others, he became a criminal while in office or after leaving the profession.

The hangman's income varied from place to place and also fluctuated from year to year, according to how much work he had to do. It generally included a small salary, together with a fee for each person he executed and any other punishment which he inflicted. The salary and fees gradually increased as the hangman's role diminished.

Perquisites enjoyed by the hangman also varied from place to place. Those of the London official included gratuities of several guineas each from noblemen and other wealthy prisoners about to be executed, the clothes of the condemned (i.e., those they wore to their executions) and any money made from the sale of his ropes.

These perquisites, together with his salary and fees, gave the holder of the London post a good income during his best years. But there were times when the number of executions he had to perform fell sharply, and his earnings then fell sharply, too. As a result, he was sometimes very poor.

Other members of the profession, however, had rent-free houses and other emoluments which were unaffected by falls in the frequency of executions. So, although their incomes were usually a lot lower than the London hangman's, their living standards were generally more secure.

In view of the horrible duties they carried out and the social ostracism they had to endure, it may well be assumed by some readers that our oldtime hangmen were all sordid and disreputable people. But that was not the case.

Their occupation was certainly low class and *some* hangmen were clearly

The whipping of an offender 'at the cart's tail' in 1656 (from a contemporary print).

unsavoury, low-life characters. Some behaved shockingly towards the condemned; some even ended up being hanged themselves. But others - perhaps most of them - were honest and inoffensive.

One Scottish hangman, at his death in 1823, was actually described in an obituary as 'an object of respect rather than aversion'. This may, of course, have been an exaggeration, but, even so, obituaries of some other executioners of the time do not give too bad an impression of their subjects.

Honest and inoffensive hangmen were obviously not as much despised as their more obnoxious brother functionaries, but were undoubtedly affected to some extent by the stigma attached to the profession as a whole. Even the writer of the 1823 obituary made clear his own distaste for the hangman's 'repulsive office'.

Yet, honest or dishonest, offensive or inoffensive, our hangmen of those days seem generally to have been of little interest to contemporary journalists - or, indeed, to contemporary writers of any sort. For although the newspapers and pamphlets of the time tell us a lot about executions and about the crimes of the condemned, they contain relatively little information about the hangmen themselves.

In many execution reports, the man who officiated at the gallows is referred to merely as 'the Common Hangman' or 'the Executioner', as though he had no personal identity. In many cases, his own death was either not reported or was announced without any details of his life or career.

Where he was regarded as more newsworthy, it was usually because he had been involved in some bizarre incident, had fallen foul of the law himself or had disgraced himself in some other way. Unfortunately, details of his background were rarely given even then.

1. Early Hangmen

During the late Middle Ages, England and Wales had many executions. A lot of them, however, seem to have been carried out by people who were not professional hangmen.

In Kent, for example, the Porter of Canterbury was at one time the county executioner. This custom was in force in the reign of Henry II (1154-89) and remained so until well into the next century. It may actually have lasted for a lot longer than that, but we have as yet no evidence that it did so. Nor does it appear to be known whether any of England's other medieval city porters performed duties of this type.

In Caernarvonshire, Merionethshire and Anglesey, in north Wales, during the first half of the fifteenth century, executions were carried out by bondmen from the King's estates. The bondmen generally had no liking for such work, but were forced to do it by their sheriffs, who were themselves responsible for ensuring that the executions were carried out.

Eventually, in 1446, Henry VI put a stop to this coercion, after receiving a petition from some of the bondmen concerned. The petition, according to a contemporary record, claimed that the practice had caused many other bondmen to flee the three counties, with the result that 'many towns are desolate and divers rents, services and pence taken away'. It also pointed out that in Flintshire, another county in north Wales, executions were carried out by the sheriffs themselves.

But whoever served as hangman for a particular county at this time, whether voluntarily or otherwise, did not usually carry out *all* of the executions which took place there. For certain towns tried and executed capital offenders themselves, in accordance with local laws or customs; so, too, did lords of manors and even abbots in some cases. This was where the right to inflict capital punishment had been granted to the town concerned - or to a manorial lord or a monastery - by the Crown, or where it had merely been assumed by some powerful individual without any grant of franchise.

In towns which had this privilege, the town bailiff was probably the official executioner, but local records show that in some cases the condemned person's accuser had to carry out the sentence (or find somebody else to do it for him). In Dover, in the fifteenth century, for example, this apparently happened in all cases except those in which the proceedings had been initiated by the Crown. In those cases, 'the baylly' had to perform the execution.

A similar situation existed in Romney at the end of that century, with the bailiff having to provide the gallows and the rope and the prosecutor the hangman.

'And if he ("the suter") may fynde non hangman neither that he wyll noght do that same office himself,' said the Romney law, 'he shall dwelle in prison with the felon unto the time that he wyll do that office or else find an hangman.'

The landowners and abbots who exercised their own right to impose the death penalty could always call upon their own bailiffs to act as executioners, and most probably did so. But on some manors different customs prevailed.

One such manor was that of Stoneley, in Warwickshire, where at one time four bondmen were each obliged by their conditions of tenure to erect a gallows and hang thieves when required to do so. Each of the four also had to plough, reap, make the lord's malt, do other servile work and wear a red clout on his upper garment, to show that he was a hangman.

In Cheshire, lords of the manor of Kinderton went on asserting their right to hang felons until almost the end of the sixteenth century: the last to suffer this form of punishment there was probably Hugh Stringer, a murderer executed in 1591. At that time, a John Croxton de Ravenscroft held lands and tenements on the manor on condition that he rendered certain services, one of which was to find a hangman when one was needed there. The person he found to hang Stringer was a man named John Lingard, who carried out the execution for five shillings.

Though executions in the late Middle Ages were mostly by hanging, other forms of capital punishment were also used. During the fourteenth century, for example, hanging, drawing and quartering became the usual penalty for men convicted of treason, while women convicted of the same offence were liable to be burnt. Members of the nobility who committed treason were, however, afforded the privilege of being beheaded instead.

Peine forte et dure, or pressing to death, was used from the early fifteenth century onwards, initially as a form of torture and then as a mode of execution.

There were also local variations, with some towns, at one time or another, drowning, burying alive or burning offenders for crimes which were punishable by hanging elsewhere. In Dover, in the fifteenth century, the condemned seem generally to have been thrown from a cliff.

Halifax at some stage began executing thieves with a decapitation machine similar to the guillotine later used in France. This device, known as the Halifax Gibbet, was used to behead offenders convicted of stealing goods valued at 13½d or more. Its earliest recorded use was in 1541, but it is believed to have been used for some centuries prior to its abandonment in 1650.

The Gibbet consisted of a wooden frame, a heavy blade attached to a sliding wooden block and a lower block on which the condemned placed his or her neck. It was operated by means of a long rope attached to a wooden pin holding the sliding block in place.

There was not normally just one executioner. Generally, the rope would be pulled by all of the men who were standing close enough to hold it, while others

An execution by the Halifax Gibbet (from an old print).

present reached out towards it, as a token that they wished to see justice done. But in cases in which the condemned had been sentenced for stealing an animal such as a horse, an ox or a sheep, another animal of the same type would have the rope tied to it and would then be driven away.

It is not known when English towns began to employ officials who were primarily executioners. The post of Common Hangman may well have existed in some towns during the Middle Ages, but so far no evidence of it has come to light.

Another possibility is that England at that time had many unofficial or peripatetic hangmen, carrying out executions wherever their services were required. Many sheriffs, bailiffs and prosecutors who would otherwise have had to perform such duties themselves would undoubtedly have been willing to pay somebody else to act in their place.

During the Tudor era, England's use of capital punishment was greater than ever before. Only a small number of crimes were then capital offences (far fewer than in the eighteenth and early nineteenth centuries), but the number of executions which actually took place reached its peak between the years 1536 and 1553, when an estimated 560 people were put to death every year at Tyburn alone. It therefore seems reasonable to assume that many men made their living as executioners, official or otherwise, at that time.

The earliest known hangman of London was a man named Cratwell or Gratnell, who held the post from 1534 to 1538. Described by a contemporary chronicler as 'a conninge butcher in quarteringe of men', Cratwell must have executed about two thousand people during his four-year tenure of office, but Anne Boleyn, who was beheaded in 1536, was not one of them. A French executioner was brought over from St Omer to perform that particular task, using a sword instead of the customary axe.

It is interesting to note that the London hangman's right to the clothes of his victims was recognized in Cratwell's time. Sir Thomas More, preparing for his execution in 1535, put on his best gown, which was made of silk, but was advised by the Lieutenant of the Tower of London that a garment of poorer quality would be good enough for the person who was to have it. More took his advice and changed into a gown made of frieze.

On 1 September 1538, Cratwell was himself hanged, along with two accomplices, for robbing a booth at Bartholomew Fair. The triple execution took place in Clerkenwell, on a newly-erected gallows, before a crowd of over 20,000 people.

We do not know who followed Cratwell as hangman of London, or for how long his successor remained in the post. But in 1541, Margaret Pole, the sixty-eight-year-old Countess of Salisbury, was beheaded at the Tower by a clumsy novice, who hacked her head and shoulders hideously before the execution was completed. It was England's worst-ever bungling of an execution of this type on record.

Twelve years later, a French ecclesiastic named Stephen Perlin witnessed the beheading of the Duke of Northumberland. He later recalled that the man who officiated on that occasion 'was lame of a leg... and... wore a white apron, like a butcher'. Like Cratwell, this lame finisher of the law, whose name is unknown, eventually ended up on the gallows himself. His execution, in 1556, was recorded by a diarist of the time as follows:

> The ij day of July rod in a care (rode in a cart) v. unto Tyborne: on was the hangman with the stump-lege for stheft (theft), wyche he had hangyd mony a man and quartered mony, and hed (beheaded) many a nobull man and odur (other).

Only one other London hangman of the sixteenth century is known to us: that was a fellow named Bull, who occupied the post in 1593. It is not known how long he had been in office by that time, but a man of the same name had beheaded Mary Queen of Scots at Fotheringhay Castle six years earlier: a task for which he was paid £10. It may well have been the same man, but we do not know for sure.

The only other thing we know about the London hangman named Bull is that he had died or left office by the early part of 1601.

By this time, many English provincial towns undoubtedly had hangmen of their own, though nothing seems to be known about any of them. A letter dated 4 July 1599 in the Chester City Records Office contains a reference to a local executioner, but it doesn't give his name, nor does it indicate whether or not he held an official post in the city. The letter, to the Mayor of Chester (apparently from the Mayor of Denbigh), requests the use of that executioner for 'some urgente busines' in Denbigh later the same week.

In towns where the hangman had an official post, the means by which he was chosen depended on local tradition. In most cases, the person appointed was probably a volunteer; some towns, however, had different customs, as is clear from information which has come to light about some of their later hangmen.

The holder of the York post was usually a pardoned felon. One of that city's eighteenth-century hangmen was Matthew Blackbourn, whose appointment is recorded in the *Gentleman's Magazine* of 1731. This tells us that at the York Assizes in March of that year three men were sentenced to death, adding: 'Matthew Blackbourn, capitally convicted at the same time, had his Pardon being made Hangman.' The other three men were all hanged.

Eight years later, on 7 April 1739, another York hangman officiated at the local gallows for the first time, hanging the legendary Dick Turpin and one other man. 'Laurence Roberts, Thomas Hadfield (who was Hangman) and Naomi Hollings, who pleaded her Belly, and were all under Sentence of Death, are repriev'd,' says the *York Courant's* report of the proceedings. Hadfield had been convicted of highway robbery.

The Taunton post was hereditary. A Captain William LeGeyt, visiting the town in 1804, recorded that the office was held by a 'poor devil' named Joshua Otway, and had been in the same family since the Bloody Assizes of 1685.* There may also have been other hereditary posts of this type in England, but, if so, we know nothing about them.

Local tradition also determined the range of duties which our hangmen were expected to perform. In some cases, these included tasks unrelated to the punishment of offenders.

In 1705, one Alexander Robinson was appointed hangman in Newcastle-upon-Tyne. A corporation record of his appointment states: 'It is ordered that he (Robinson) be settled in the room of Thomas Cooper and be common executioner in hanging of felons, putting persons in the pillory(,) in scourging the poor, clearing the streets of swine and to do and perform all other matters belonging to

---

* A copy of LeGeyt's journal, or part of it, is contained in unpublished notes on the town by L. E. J. Brooke, held in the Somerset Studies Library, Taunton.

An execution by the Maiden (from *The Malefactor's Register*, 1779).

the place and duty of the hangman.'

John Sykes and T. Fordyce tell us, in *Local Records* (1866-76), that the Newcastle hangman in Robinson's time was known locally as the *Whipper and Hougher*. This, they say, was from his having to whip delinquents and 'cut the houghs, or sinews of the houghs' of the swine that infested the town.

In Scotland, from medieval times, rich and powerful landowners enjoyed baronial rights, enabling them (like many English lords of manors) to try and execute capital offenders on their own estates. Baron courts continued to dispense justice in some parts of Scotland until they were abolished in 1747, with some families retaining their own hangmen until at least the seventeenth century. Unfortunately, we know nothing about the conditions of service of any of these private executioners.

Many Scottish towns at this time had full-time hangmen with official posts. These, like their English counterparts, inflicted whippings and other minor punishments, in addition to the executions they carried out. Some also served as dempsters (or doomsters): court officers who pronounced sentence on prisoners convicted of capital crimes. In most cases, they appear to have been provided with a free house at the town's expense, as well as receiving a salary and fees.

Most of the executions which took place in Scotland in the sixteenth and seventeenth centuries were by hanging; but, as in England, other methods were also used. Some offenders were strangled and then burnt; some were burnt alive; some were drowned; some were beheaded. At one time, it had been customary for women to be drowned rather than hanged, because drowning was considered more respectful to them.

In Edinburgh, between 1565 and 1710, some 120 people were beheaded by a machine called the Maiden. This had been constructed on the orders of the Earl of Morton, who had seen the Halifax Gibbet in operation and been impressed by its efficiency. Unlike the Gibbet, the Maiden was used only for the execution of persons of rank. Morton himself was beheaded by it in 1581.

Scottish hangmen of this time were often called *lockmen*. The origin of this word is thought to lie in a privilege enjoyed by the Edinburgh functionary of taking a *lock*, or handful, of meal from every sack of this commodity exposed for sale in the city market. Many Scottish executioners appear to have had perquisites of this type during the period under consideration, and in some cases they were of far greater value than the Edinburgh hangman's.

In Stirling, in the seventeenth century, the hangman was known as the *Staffman*, and it has been suggested that this was because his appointment was marked by the presentation of a staff of office. One occupant of the post was Thomas Grant, who was appointed in 1633, having previously served as private executioner to the Laird of Glenalmond, in Perthshire. Grant's appointment to the Stirling post was for life and his absence from the town without the permission of his employers was punishable by death, as is shown in the following extract from the Burgh Records:

20 May, 1633. - Thomas Grant, borne in Glenalmond, under David Murray of Bulhindye, ressavit and sworne servand and executionar to this town of Stirling his lyfe tyme, and sall not remove nor absent himself aff the toune, but license of the Magistrats, under the pane of daithe.

Grant was not unique in accepting such a bizarre condition of service: John McClelland, a Glasgow hangman, did the same at *his* appointment in 1605. McClelland, however, was a capital offender who, like Matthew Blackbourn and Thomas Hadfield, agreed to become hangman in order to avoid being hanged himself. Grant appears not to have been in any trouble at all.

2. Father and Son

At the beginning of the seventeenth century, a man named Derrick was hangman of London. It was he who beheaded the Earl of Essex in 1601; Guy Fawkes and seven other Gunpowder Plot conspirators, who were hanged, drawn and quartered five years later, were almost certainly among his victims as well. It is not known when he acceded to the post, but he seems to have become quite a wellknown character during the course of his career.

There are references to Derrick in several tracts published in the early years of James I's reign, and it was about this time that the word *derrick* came into use, meaning a hangman, a hanging, a gallows or a gibbet. Various authors have claimed that the crane known as a derrick was so named because it is similar in shape to the gallows on which Derrick hanged his victims, but this is not so.

The main London gallows in Derrick's time was the Triple Tree at Tyburn: a large triangular structure to which the crane in question bears no real resemblance at all. It is, however, quite feasible that the crane was called a derrick because of its similarity to a gibbet, after the gibbet itself had become known by that name.

It has also been repeatedly claimed that Derrick the hangman had once been under sentence of death for rape and that it was Essex himself who had saved him from the gallows. This had allegedly happened while Derrick was serving under Essex in Spain (or in France, according to some accounts). The source of the story is a contemporary ballad in which Essex, at his own execution, addresses Derrick as follows:

'Derrick, thou know'st at Cales I sav'd
  Thy life, lost for a rape there done;
Where thou thyself can'st testify
  Thine own hand three-and-twenty hung.'

But that is hardly a reliable source of information, and we have no other evidence to corroborate it. In fact, we have no real evidence that Derrick ever served under Essex at all.

Derrick, like all holders of his post, was hangman not only to the City of London but to the County of Middlesex as well. The number of people he executed is unknown, but it was almost certainly well over a hundred a year (the annual average for Middlesex alone was 73.6 during the years 1608-17 and it was probably about the same during the previous few years). There were also many whippings inflicted by the hangman 'at the cart's tail' at this time.

Another duty which Derrick would have performed regularly was the branding of prisoners who escaped the death penalty by pleading 'benefit of clergy'. This

The hanging, drawing and quartering of some of the Gunpowder Plot conspirators
(from a contemporary Dutch engraving).

medieval privilege was not afforded to female prisoners in Derrick's time, but
males convicted of all but a small number of 'non-clergyable' offences, such as
high treason, could claim it - even murderers.

A prisoner wishing to do so had only to 'seek the book' before sentence was
passed on him and prove his literacy by reading the first verse of the 51st Psalm
(the 'Neck Verse', as it was often called) to the prison chaplain:

> Have mercy upon me, O God, according to thy loving kindness: according unto
> the multitude of thy tender mercies blot out my transgressions.

If he could do this, it would be accepted that he 'read as a clerk' and his life
would be spared.

The custom was farcical, for many illiterate criminals knew the Neck Verse off
by heart and were able to claim the privilege merely by pretending that they could
read. Laymen, however, were legally entitled to claim benefit of clergy only once,
and, having done so, would be branded on the left thumb ('burnt in the hand') by
the hangman, to show that they had already availed themselves of it. Branding
was also used as a punishment in itself at this time, and for a long time
afterwards.

Derrick apparently did not always perform his duties satisfactorily, for it is known that he was flogged on one occasion - this was on 12 July 1606 - for failing to brand a prisoner in Newgate earlier the same day. The flogging was carried out at Bridewell, the house of correction.

It is not known when Derrick's tenure of office ended or when the next known hangman of London, Gregory Brandon, was appointed to the post. The earliest references to Brandon appear in the Middlesex Sessions Records for 1611, which show that in February of that year he was himself convicted of a capital offence but successfully pleaded benefit of clergy. These records were originally written mostly in Latin, but an unpublished English version edited by W. J. Hardy and William Le Hardy gives details of Brandon's conviction as follows:

> Gregory Brandon, of London, yeoman, for assaulting Simon Mooreton at Whitechapple and wounding him with 'a hanger' (a short sword) so that he died. Guilty. No goods. Seeks the book. Reads as a clerk. Branded with the letter T. (for Tyburn) and delivered according to the form of the statute. Indicted of homicide.

The same work gives details of recognizances which Brandon and two other men entered into in connection with this affair, the editors in this case showing that they believed Brandon was already the hangman by this time:

> Gregory Brandon, of Rosemarilane (the hangman), John Williams, of the same, labourer, and John Turner, of the same, 'fisher', for the same Gregory to keep the peace towards Thomas Regnolds (*sic*), of Rosemarilane, barber-surgeon. Handed over.

A further item about recognizances shows that on 16 September of the same year Brandon stood surety for his wife and two other women from the same street (one of whom appears to have been Simon Mooreton's widow), evidently as a result of a disturbance of some sort:

> Gregory Brandon of Rosemary Lane, yeoman, for Alice his wife, Alice Morton

Women were allowed to claim benefit of clergy for certain minor capital offences from 1622 onwards, and for the same crimes as men from 1692. During the course of the eighteenth century, however, the privilege became progressively less important, due to big increases in the number of crimes which were made capital offences 'without benefit of clergy'. The reading of the Neck Verse was discontinued in 1705, and benefit of clergy was itself abolished in 1827 (except for peers and peeresses, who were entitled to claim it in some cases up to 1841).

and Agnes Tanner, both of the same, widows, to keep the peace.

It is odd to find Brandon standing surety for Alice Morton and Agnes Tanner, as both of these women are included in the list of witnesses on the indictment on which he had been tried (as is Thomas Reynolds).

There are further references to both Gregory Brandon and his wife in the Middlesex Sessions Records for 1615. In April of that year, Robert Dewer, also of Rosemary Lane, Whitechapel, yeoman, was tried for stealing a counterpoint worth £20 and acquitted. Alice Brandon was one of two prosecutors in this case, the other being a man named Henry Porter.

The following month, Gregory Brandon accused a sailor named Thomas Nicholas, another resident of Rosemary Lane, of stealing three keys, a chain and a pair of gloves from him. In this case, the prosecution was apparently dropped.

Finally, towards the end of November, Gregory and Alice were indicted, along with another couple, for helping and receiving three thieves after they had stolen two carpets, eleven pieces of pewter and various other articles. Gregory was tried for the crime and acquitted, but Alice, who is recorded as having been 'at large', seems not to have been tried at all.

A year after his acquittal, Gregory Brandon was granted a coat of arms as a result of a trick played on the Garter King of Arms, Sir William Segar, by a rival herald. The incident was recorded in a letter written by George Carew, the Earl of Totnes, in January 1617, which tells us:

> York Herald played a trick on Garter King-at-Arms, by sending him a coat-of-arms drawn up for Gregory Brandon, said to be a merchant of London, and well descended, which Garter subscribed, and then found that Brandon was the hangman; Garter and York are both imprisoned, one for foolery, the other for knavery.

The trick had allegedly been devised by York (Ralph Brooke) in a deliberate attempt to discredit Garter.

It has been suggested that Brandon and his successors were popularly given the title of 'Esquire' as a result of this affair, but there are no real grounds for believing this. The title *was* bestowed on some of our later London hangmen in pamphlets and newspapers, though only in a few cases. Where it *did* happen, it was probably done just out of facetiousness.

Gregory Brandon continued as hangman until his death - about 1639 - when his son Richard (sometimes called 'Young Gregory') succeeded him. During his last years, when Richard is believed to have served as his assistant, the number of executions he carried out was considerably lower than it had been at the beginning of his career.

The number of Middlesex prisoners executed during the fifteen years 1625-39 was 568 or thereabouts: an annual average of about 37.8, or little more than half of what it had been in 1608-17. This reduction, of course, meant fewer fees and suits of clothes for the hangman, and it is likely that the number of London executions fell similarly during the same period. Gregory Brandon's standard of living must therefore have been quite a bit lower in the second half of his career than it had been in the first.

Richard Brandon was hangman of London for about ten years and was allegedly the executioner of Charles I. He died at his home in Rosemary Lane on 20 June 1649.

A contemporary pamphlet, *The Last Will and Testament of Richard Brandon Esquire* (1649), describes him as 'a lewd and notorious villain' and says that he had twice been sentenced to death for bigamy. It also says that he had prepared himself for his calling by killing cats and dogs and that he claimed the gallows 'by inheritance' when his father died.

The allegation that he had twice been sentenced to death is partially corroborated by an earlier tract, *The Organ's Eccho*, which suggests that he was committed for trial for bigamy in 1641. It must, however, be said that this is not borne out by any of the Middlesex Sessions Records which have so far been translated, which contain no evidence that he was ever charged with any crime.

Richard Brandon's many victims included the Earl of Strafford in 1641 and Archbishop Laud in 1645, both of whom were beheaded on Tower Hill. On his deathbed, he allegedly confessed that he was also the man who had beheaded Charles I: an execution which he had initially said he would not carry out.

Charles was executed on a scaffold in Whitehall on 30 January 1649, by one masked man assisted by another. Executions carried out by Brandon after that include those of the Earl of Holland, the Duke of Hamilton and Lord Capel.

Brandon's alleged confession is described in some detail in another pamphlet, published towards the end of June 1649. *The Confession of Richard Brandon* also makes certain claims about the circumstances of the hangman's death and his burial in St Mary's Churchyard, Whitechapel, the following day:

Upon Wednesday last (being the 20. of this instant June, 1649) Richard Brandon, the late Executioner and Hang-man, who beheaded his late Majesty, King of Great Brittain, departed this life; But during the time of his sicknesse, his Conscience was much troubled, and exceedingly perplexed in mind, yet little shew of repentance, for remission of his sins, and by past transgressions, which had so much power and influence upon him, that he seemed to live in them, and they in him. And upon Sunday last, a young man of his acquaintance going in to visit him, fell into discourse, asked him how he did, and whether he was not troubled in conscience for cutting off of the Kings head?

He replyed, yes! by reason that (upon the time of his tryall, and at the

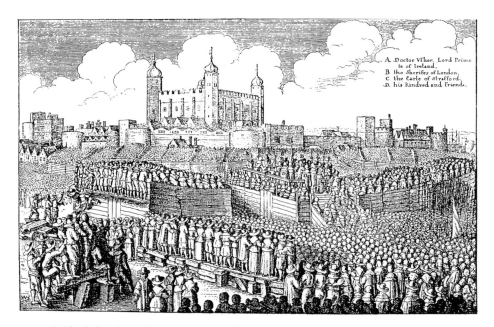

The beheading of the Earl of Strafford by Richard Brandon in 1641 (from a contemporary Dutch print).

denouncing of Sentence against him) he had taken a vow and protestation, Wishing God to perish him body and soul, if ever he appeared on the scaffold to do the act or lift up his hand against him.

Further acknowledging, That he was no sooner entred upon the scaffold, but immediatly he fell a trembling, and hath ever since continued in the like agony.

He likewise confessed, that he had 30. pounds for his pains, all paid him in half Crowns, within an hour after the blow was given, and that he had an Orenge stuck full of Cloves, and a handkircher out of the Kings pocket, so soon as he was carryed off from the Scaffold, for which Orenge, he was proffered 20. shillings by a Gentleman in Whitehall, but refused the same, and afterwards sold it for ten s. in Rose-mary Lane.

About 6 of the clock at night, he returned home to his wife living in Rose-mary lane, and gave her the money, saying, That it was the deerest money that ever he earn'd in his life, for it would cost him his life. Which propheticall words were soon made manifest; for it appeared, that ever since he hath been in a most sad condition, and upon the Almighties first scourging of him with the Rod of meeknesse, and the friendly admonition of divers friends, for the calling of him to repentance, yet he persisted on in his vicious Vices, and would not hearken thereunto, but lay raging and swearing, and still pointing at one thing or another, which he conceived to appear visible before him.

About three dayes before he dy'd he lay speechlesse, uttering many a sigh and heavy groan, and so in a most desparing manner departed from his bed of sorrow. For the buriall whereof, great store of Wines were sent in, by the Sheriff of the City of London, and a great multitude of people stood wayting to see his Corps carryed to the Church-yard; some crying out, Hang him Rogue, bury him in the Dung-hill; others pressing upon him, saying, They would quarter him, for executing of the King; Insomuch, that the Church-wardens and Masters of the Parish were fain to come for the suppressing of them, and (with great difficulty) he was at last carryed to White chappell Church-yard, having (as it is said) a bunch of Rosemary at each end of the coffin, on the top thereof, with a Rope tyed crosse from one end to the other.

And a merry conceited Cook living at the sign of the Crown, having a black Fan (worth the value of 30 shilings) took a resolution to rent the same in pieces, and to every feather tyed a piece of pack-thread dy'd in black Ink, and gave them to divers persons, who (in derision) for a while, wore them in their hats.

In a concluding paragraph, the *Confession* tells us that the hangman's assistant at the King's execution was a ragman who also lived in Rosemary Lane. Another account of Brandon's death, in the *Kingdoms Weekly Intelligencer* of 19-26 June, makes the same claim, giving the man's name as Ralph Jones. The *Intelligencer's* report ends by naming William Loe, 'a dust carrier and cleaner of the dung hills', as the new executioner.

Brandon's burial, on 21 June, was recorded in the Parish Register of St Mary's as follows:

21st. Rich. Brandon, a man out of Rosemary Lane.

And to this was later added a marginal note in a different hand:

This R. Brandon is supposed to have cut off the head of Charles the first.

The addition is unlikely to have been made before the Restoration, as the dead king would not have been called Charles I until the accession of Charles II.

Nine days after Brandon's death, the new hangman of London, William Low (or Loe, or Lowen), hanged twenty-four offenders at Tyburn, eight from each beam of the Triple Tree. This was the largest number that could be hanged there at any one time without any of the bodies touching those alongside them.

Low remained hangman until his own death, which took place on or about 12 August 1653.

* * *

Like the *Confession*, the *Last Will and Testament* and one other contemporary tract, *A Dialogue, or a Dispute between the Late Hangman and Death* (1649), both claim that Richard Brandon was the man who beheaded Charles I. So, too, does the *Intelligencer's* report of the hangman's own death and burial.

Yet, following the Restoration, an Ironside named William Hulet was accused of the deed and put on trial. In his own defence, Hulet tried to prove that Brandon was the real culprit, but was convicted and sentenced to death. It is not known whether he was executed or pardoned.

Hulet's conviction, at any rate, shows that the evidence pointing to Brandon as the King's executioner was far from conclusive. Had it been stronger, then Hulet would obviously not have been accused in the first place.

Brandon was, in fact, just one of a number of men accused or suspected, at one time or another, of having struck the fatal blow. The truth is that we do not know who struck it and that Brandon's alleged confession may well have been a complete fabrication.

3. The Original Jack Ketch

The next known hangman of London after William Low was Edward Dunn, whose name appears in the Middlesex Sessions Records for 1657. These show that in October of that year four thieves were apprehended after breaking into Dunn's own house, which is said by a contemporary pamphlet to have been in or near Golden Lane, Cripplegate. The pamphlet, *The Devils Cabinet Broke Open* (1658), claims that the hangman's house was actually a regular meeting place for a criminal gang about that time, but there appears to be no evidence of this anywhere else. And Dunn himself seems never to have been prosecuted for any offence.

It is, however, clear that he was already the hangman by October 1657 - the Sessions Records refer to him as 'Edward Dunn executioner' - and he is also known to have been still in office at his death on 11 September 1663. He must therefore have held the post for at least six years and carried out executions for treason both before and after the Restoration. And those which he performed during the reign of Charles II undoubtedly included the hanging, drawing and quartering of some of Charles I's judges and other prominent supporters of the Commonwealth.*

One such execution was that of John Cooke and Hugh Peters, who suffered this ghastly fate together in October 1660. A contemporary account of the deaths of these two men leaves us in little doubt that their executioner derived pleasure from his horrible occupation. The account states:

> When Mr. Cook was cut down, and brought to be Quartered, one they called Col. Turner, called to the Sheriffs men, to bring Mr. Peters near, that he might see it; And by and by the Hangman came to him all besmeared in Blood, and rubbing his bloody hands together, he (tauntingly) asked, Come, how do you like this Mr. Peters, how do you like this work? To whom he replyed, I am not (I thank God) terrified at it, you may do your worst.

The following year, Thomas Ellwood, a Quaker and a friend of Milton, witnessed a shocking incident involving Dunn at Newgate Prison. Dunn had

---

* The term *hanged, drawn and quartered* is not strictly accurate, as, contrary to popular belief, the word 'drawn' merely signifies that the condemned were pulled to the place of execution on sledges or hurdles, rather than taken in carts like other prisoners: the correct order of the words is therefore *drawn, hanged and quartered.* For this reason, some writers prefer to use the term *hanged, disembowelled and quartered* to describe this frightful form of execution.

arrived at the prison to parboil the severed heads of three other men who had been executed in the same way, prior to their being displayed in prominent positions in the City. This is how Ellwood later described what happened:

> I saw the Heads, when they were brought up to be Boyled. The Hangman fetch'd them in a dirty Dust Basket, out of some By-Place; and setting them down amongst the Felons, he and they made Sport with them. They took them by the Hair, Flouting, Jeering and Laughing at them: and then giving them some ill Names, box'd them on the Ears and Cheeks.

Only then, according to Ellwood, did the hangman set about the task of parboiling them.

When prisoners were sentenced to be hanged, drawn and quartered, the sentence invariably directed that they should be cut down for disembowelling while still alive. In practice, however, they were often not cut down until they were dead, or at least insensible.

In one particular case, Dunn allegedly visited a prisoner due to undergo this form of execution and demanded money from him, threatening to 'torture him exceedingly' if he did not get £5. The condemned man, John James, was very poor and could give him nothing, but the hangman's threat was not carried out. John James was left to hang until he was dead, probably on the orders of the sheriffs.

There are references to Dunn by name in several contemporary publications, including the satirist Samuel Butler's *Proposals for forming Liberty of Conscience* (1663), in which he is described as an 'uncircumcised Philistine'. Another, an anonymous tract entitled *Groanes from Newgate; or, An Elegy upon Edward Dun, Esq., the Cities' Common Hangman* (also published in 1663), gives the date of his death and informs us that he died naturally in his bed.

This, however, is all that is known about him, and we have no record of the appointment of his successor. The next occupant of the London post of whom anything is known was Jack Ketch, the most infamous hangman of all.

* * *

The earliest known references to Ketch appear in tracts published in 1678. It is clear from these that he was already an established figure by this time and, in the absence of any evidence to the contrary, some writers have assumed that he was Dunn's immediate successor. But this may not be true at all: there may actually have been two or three other London hangmen between Dunn and himself.

Ketch, at any rate, held the office for most of the period 1678-86, during which time he gained a shocking reputation for both savagery and incompetence.

A hanging at Tyburn about 1680 (from a contemporary print).

Following his death, his name became the traditional name for the hangman in many parts of the country, and remained so until well into the nineteenth century. It is still in use even today as the name of the hangman in Punch-and-Judy shows.

Ketch - or Catch, as he was sometimes called - was the executioner of many innocent Roman Catholics who were put to death as a result of the 'Popish Plot' conspiracy of 1678. His known victims also included those executed for the Rye House Plot of 1683 and the Duke of Monmouth, who was beheaded in 1685.

On one occasion, Ketch carried out an execution in Oxford: that of Stephen College, the 'Protestant Joiner', who was hanged, drawn and quartered on 31 August 1681. It has been claimed that he also executed rebels in the West Country during the Bloody Assizes, but there appears to be no evidence of this.

Ketch's reputation for bungling began with the execution of Lord William Russell, who was beheaded on a scaffold in Lincoln's Inn Fields on 21 July 1683. It is not clear how bad a case this was, for the details vary according to which account we read. One, by Sir Charles Lyttelton, an eyewitness, states: 'The hangman gave him 3 blows, besides sawing wth ye ax, before he cut his head of.' But Bishop Gilbert Burnet, who was also present (and was a friend of Russell's) tells us in his *History of My Own Time* that the prisoner's head was 'cut off at two strokes'.

Whatever the truth of the matter, the execution was followed by the publication of a pamphlet, *The Apologie of John Ketch Esq.*, ostensibly written by the hangman himself in vindication of his performance - 'since it is not fit that so Publick a Person as the Executioner of Justice... should lye under the scandal of untrue Reports, and be unjustly Expos'd to popular Clamour'.

In the pamphlet, Ketch dismisses as untrue allegations that he bungled the execution through being drunk, or struck ineffective blows on purpose, to cause needless suffering to his victim. He also denies a rumour that when the first blow proved ineffectual, Russell said to him, 'You dog! Did I give you ten guineas to use me so inhumanly?' He even denies that ten guineas was the sum which Russell gave him.

The pamphlet was probably not intended to serve any serious purpose and certainly did not put a stop to the rumours of the hangman's incompetence. In fact, it may well have done just the opposite.

In 1685, Titus Oates, the inventor of the 'Popish Plot', was whipped through the streets from Aldgate to Newgate, following his conviction for perjury: this was on 20 May. Two days later, he was whipped again, this time from Newgate to Tyburn.

Both whippings were inflicted by Jack Ketch, with the utmost severity. On the first occasion, the offender was whipped at the cart's tail; on the second, he was

The whipping of Titus Oates from Aldgate to Newgate (from a contemporary Dutch print).

dragged on a sledge, becoming, says the historian Laurence Echard, 'a dismal and piteous Spectacle to the People, who cou'd much better judge of his Punishment, than his Crimes'.

'In sum, as he himself says, he sustain'd unexpressible Torments; and his escaping with Life was insisted on by his Friends as something miraculous, and a signal Testimony of his Innocence,' concludes Echard.

The beheading of the Duke of Monmouth, Ketch's most famous victim, took place less than two months after those two revolting spectacles. And his performance on that occasion was far worse than it had been at the execution of Lord Russell.

The 'Protestant Duke' was executed on Tower Hill on 15 July, before a large crowd of spectators. As at Russell's execution (and also those of Essex and Charles I), a low block was used: one before which the prisoner had to lie full length rather than kneel. The scaffold was draped with black cloth, as was usual at executions of this type.

In view of Ketch's reputation, Monmouth was understandably apprehensive. 'Here are six guineas for you,' he said, handing Ketch the money. 'Pray do your business well. Don't serve me as you did my Lord Russell. I have heard you struck him three or four times.' He then gave some other coins to his servant, who was with him on the scaffold, saying, 'Here, take these remaining guineas and give them to him if he does his work well.'

'I hope I shall,' said Ketch.

'If you strike me twice, I cannot promise you not to stir,' warned the prisoner.

Taking off his coat and periwig, Monmouth then lay down and placed his neck on the block, but suddenly raised himself on his elbow. 'Prithee, let me feel the axe,' he said. The hangman let him feel it, but the Duke then said, 'I fear it is not sharp enough.'

'It is sharp enough and heavy enough,' insisted Ketch.

Making no further comment, Monmouth put his neck back onto the block. Four clergymen who were attending him prayed fervently, commending his spirit and his soul to God. The crowd watched silently as the axe was raised.

But Ketch had apparently been unnerved by Monmouth's remark about Russell's execution, for he brought the axe down distractedly, inflicting only a slight wound in the Duke's neck. Monmouth raised his head and turned to look at him, as if to upbraid him, but lay down again without saying anything.

Ketch then struck a second blow, which made only a deeper gash; then, in desperation, a third, which also failed to cut off Monmouth's head. To the horror of the spectators, he then threw down the axe, exclaiming, 'God damn me, I can do no more! My heart fails me!'

The two sheriffs forced him to pick it up and finish his work, but two more strokes were needed, and even then Ketch had to complete the decapitation with a knife. The crowds were so shocked by his conduct that he afterwards had to be protected from them.

* * *

There is no truth in the claim made by some authors that the name Jack Ketch is a corruption of Jacquet. The hangman's real name was John Ketch, as we know from his burial record (he was buried at St James's Churchyard, Clerkenwell), and there are no real grounds for suggesting otherwise. We also know, from the same source, that his last address was in Spread Eagle Alley, which, according to Edward Hatton's *New View of London* (1708), was on the north side of Bow Street, near the south end of King Street, Westminster.

It appears from a tract published in 1679, *The Man of Destiny's hard Fortune*, that Ketch had at that time recently been imprisoned for debt, but we have no reason to think that he was ever involved in crime and there is no evidence even to justify the *Dictionary of National Biography's* assertion that he once went on strike for higher wages.

He was, however, a disagreeable person, not above making his feelings known when he received a gratuity which fell short of his expectations. This happened on 7 December 1683, when Algernon Sidney was beheaded on Tower Hill: Ketch was initially given only three guineas, but after a scene this was increased to four or five guineas.

Early in 1686, Ketch was committed to Bridewell and removed from office, his place being taken by a man named Pascha Rose. Narcissus Luttrell, a contemporary diarist, recorded the event, noting that the action was taken against the hangman for 'affronting the sherifs of London'. Unfortunately, the nature of the offending act is unknown.

Pascha Rose was a butcher by trade. J. G. Muddiman, in *The Bloody Assizes* (1929), claims that he was also Ketch's assistant, but this may be just speculation. It is, however, known that at the time of his appointment, he was himself facing prosecution for a minor offence.

The Middlesex Sessions Records, where he is described merely as a labourer, show that Rose was indicted at the County Quarter Sessions on 12 January 1686 for speaking 'scandalous words' against Charles Osborne, a local justice of the peace, with the intention of bringing him into hatred and contempt. The words in question - 'God damn Justice Osborne! I am sorry I had not a razor for him!' - had allegedly been spoken within the hearing of several witnesses in Whitechapel on 18 December previously.

Rose admitted the offence and was thereupon fined £3 6s 8d and sentenced to be whipped at the cart's tail from the west end of Rosemary Lane to the nearby Hermitage Bridge. The court also ordered that he be kept in prison until he had paid the fine, undergone the whipping and found sureties for his good behaviour for twelve months.

On 20 January, a double hanging was carried out at Tyburn. It was probably Rose who carried it out, for a tract printed just two days later refers to him as the 'new Jack Catch'. This was almost certainly the first time that Ketch's name (or its accepted variation) was applied to another hangman.

The tract, *A Pleasant Discourse by way of Dialogue, between the Old and New Jack Catch,* tells us that Rose's own sentence of whipping was inflicted on the 21st. In the imaginary dialogue inspired by the event, Ketch mocks the new hangman over his 'race' from Rosemary Lane to the Hermitage and goes on to give him this advice:

Then henceforth learn for to be wise,
  Or else't may worser be;
Consider in good manners lyes,
  Your place o'th Tripple-tree:
The low Capers already you
  Have most gentiely cut
Beware the high one ben't your due,
  And I shall tye the knot.

In view of this fictitious warning, what subsequently happened to Ketch and his successor in real life was quite remarkable.

Five weeks after he was whipped, Pascha Rose was granted a free pardon. But two months later, while still holding the post of hangman, he was apprehended for a more serious offence.

This time, he and another man, Edward Smith, had broken into a house in Stepney during the daytime and stolen various articles of apparel, together valued at 20s. The two men had been seen and pursued by a neighbour of the victim, and Smith had dropped some of the stolen goods as they tried to make their escape. When they were captured, the rest of the goods were found in the hangman's breeches.

Pascha Rose and Edward Smith were tried for the crime at the Old Bailey Sessions of 20-22 May and were both found guilty. They were sentenced to death. Not long afterwards, Narcissus Luttrell recorded in his diary:

The 28th (May), five men of those lately condemned at the sessions were executed at Tyburn; one of them was one Pascha Rose, the new hangman, so that now Ketch is restored to his place.

*   *   *

Ketch outlived Rose by only a few months, dying towards the end of November. His burial took place on the 29th of that month.

A letter from a Dr Hutton to Thomas Comber, the Dean of Durham, dated 4 December, states:

> Mr. Johnson was whipped on Wednesday (1 December), but civilly used by the new hangman, Jack Ketch being buried two days before.

The identity of this new, less brutal, hangman is not known.

4. Scions of an Illustrious Family

On 1 July 1681, following the death of his predecessor, one Alexander Cockburn was appointed hangman of Edinburgh. Cockburn had previously been hangman of Stirling, having there succeeded a man named Mackenzie, whom he had somehow undermined and got dismissed from office. It is unclear from existing records whether he was still hangman of Stirling when the Edinburgh post became vacant.

Cockburn, at any rate, was not destined to hold his new post for long, for he soon fell foul of the law himself. In January 1682, he was brought to trial before the Lord Provost and bailies of Edinburgh (the city magistrates), accused of the murder of John Adamson, a licensed beggar. The Provost and bailies, as Sheriff and sheriffs-depute, had the power to try murderers who had been caught red-handed.

The crime had allegedly been committed in the hangman's own house. Cockburn denied that Adamson had been in his house that day, but it was proved that he had been. The court was also told that bloody clothes had been found in the house and that groans had been heard coming from it. Cockburn was convicted and sentenced to death.

His execution, which took place four days later, was carried out by Mackenzie, the very man he had undermined in Stirling. Cockburn died without making a confession and his body was afterwards hung in chains. His wife, Bessie Gall, was banished from the city.

The Edinburgh hangman, like most of Scotland's other municipal execution-ers, was generally called the *Lockman*, while the Stirling functionary was called the *Staffman* (see p.11). But the Edinburgh hangman sometimes had an assistant, who, as it happens, was also called the *Staffman*.

Entries in the Register of Marriages for the Parish of Edinburgh and the Register of Interments in the Greyfriars Burying-Ground show that John White, who was hangman of Edinburgh before Cockburn, had been the staffman in 1667 and 1668. Subsequent entries in the Register of Interments show that he had been appointed to the post of hangman by August 1673.

Cockburn's successor as hangman of Edinburgh was not Mackenzie but a man named Donald Monro (or Munro), who was dismissed from office two and a half years later. At the time of his dismissal, however, Monro had a staffman named Mackenzie, who was dismissed with him, so perhaps this was the same man.

Sir John Lauder's *Historical Notices of Scotish Affairs* (1848) records the dismissal of the two men as follows:

Monro, hangman of Edinburgh, and Mackeinzie his stafman, beats a poor beggar
so, that he was in hazard of his life, wheron they ware deprived, and thrust into the
theiff's hole (the common prison); (ther predecessor, Cockburne, on the 16 of
Januar 1682, was hang'd for killing a beggar.*) And one called Ormiston is
created hangman.

Monro's dismissal is also recorded in the Town Council Minutes for 20 August
1684, the date of Ormiston's appointment, where it is stated that he was deposed
for 'many miscarriages'.

John Ormiston, described elsewhere by Lauder** as a 'well favoured, discreet
fellow', was actually a scion of an illustrious family: a man with a pedigree. It is
not known where or when he was born, but his father, Robert Ormiston, had
owned an estate in Dalkeith during the first two decades of the century. Details of
the family's ancestry are to be found in *The Ormistons of Teviotdale* by Thomas
Lane Ormiston, published in 1951.

John lived for over twenty years (1652-73) in Haddington, and for short
periods in Inveresk, Fogo, Westruther and Cranston before settling in Edinburgh
in 1684. He was married three times and had sixteen children, several of whom
died young. The first child was Isabell, born in Haddington in 1652; the last was
Helen, born in Cranston in 1684.

Despite his ancestry, John Ormiston may never have been wealthy. His father,
who had been in trouble with the law for debt, is known to have parted with his
estate in 1619, so the family may have been in reduced circumstances before John
was even born. If not, then its circumstances must have become reduced during
his lifetime, for on arrival in Edinburgh, John was so poor that he accepted
employment as a servant to Robert Mowbray, the Keeper of the Correction
House. It was after this that the post of hangman became vacant.

Hangings in Edinburgh during the late seventeenth century were generally,
though not invariably, carried out in the Grassmarket. A massive block of
sandstone, known as the Gallows Stone, stood at the east end of the street and
served as a scaffold, a gibbet being erected on it whenever it was needed for this
purpose. Other hangings were carried out at the Market Cross.

Like most other hangmen of his time, the Edinburgh functionary did not just
carry out executions: he also inflicted lesser punishments, such as public
whipping and exposure in the pillory. Cockburn's first official task was the
burning of a quantity of English clothes which had been brought into the country

---

* Lauder acted as an assessor at Cockburn's trial. He tells us in another work, *The
Decisions of the Lords of Council and Session* (1759-61), that the trial took place on 16
January and the execution on the 20th.
** See *Chronological Notes of Scottish Affairs* (1822), edited by Sir Walter Scott.

By courtesy of Edinburgh City Libraries

Edinburgh's Grassmarket on Execution Day (an etching based on a watercolour by James Skene, 1775-1864).

In the seventeenth century, Scottish law allowed the punishment for certain types of murder to include mutilation, either before or after the culprit's death. One case in which this aggravated form of hanging was used was that of Phillip Stanfield, who was executed at Edinburgh's Market Cross on 24 February 1688 for the murder of his father.

Stanfield's sentence was that he be hanged until dead, then his tongue cut out and burnt, his right hand cut off and his body afterwards gibbeted. In his case, the hanging itself proved to be a grotesque spectacle, for the rope slipped so far that the condemned man's knees touched the scaffold.

The hangman brought his suffering to an end by strangling him, then carried out the rest of his ghastly sentence.

A few days after the body had been hung in chains, it was removed from the gibbet and left lying in a nearby ditch. It was then hung up again, but afterwards taken down a second time. This time it was taken away and no trace of it was ever found.

illegally. The burning was carried out at the Cross shortly after his appointment.

John Ormiston presumably carried out his duties more satisfactorily than Monro, for he continued as hangman until his death four years later, probably assisted by his young son George, who was to follow in his footsteps.

He died in December 1688 and was buried in Greyfriars Churchyard. His burial record gives his occupation as 'hangman', though the word *lockman* was normally used in Edinburgh's parish registers at that time.

No contemporary account of Ormiston's death has come to light, but an article by Robert Chambers, published in 1834, suggests that he may have committed suicide.

The article, entitled 'Scottish Executioners', appeared in *Chambers's Edinburgh Journal* on 22 February 1834. It does not mention Ormiston by name, but describes one Edinburgh hangman of the late seventeenth century as 'a reduced gentleman, the last of a respectable family who had possessed an estate in the neighbourhood of Melrose'. It is clear from his *Domestic Annals of Scotland* (1858) that Chambers believed this 'reduced gentleman' to be the person who succeeded Monro in 1684, but mistakenly believed his name to be George Ormiston.

The article claims that the 'reduced gentleman' had been profligate in his youth and had squandered his inheritance, so that eventually - 'for the sake of subsistence' - he was compelled to accept the post of hangman of Edinburgh.

'Notwithstanding his extreme degradation, this unhappy reprobate could not altogether forget his original station, and his former tastes and habits,' the article continues.

He would occasionally resume the garb of a gentleman, and mingle in the parties of citizens who played at golf in the evenings on Bruntsfield Links. Being at length recognised, he was chased from the ground with shouts of execration and loathing, which affected him so much, that he retired to the solitude of the King's Park, and was next day found dead at the bottom of a precipice, over which he appeared to have thrown himself in his despair. This rock was afterwards called the *Hangman's Craig*.

The story, which Chambers also included in two of his books, is clearly not accurate in all its details. Though the hangman in question was undoubtedly related to the Ormistons of Melrose, he was not himself descended from that branch of the family; nor was he the last of the line, as Chambers claims; nor, for that matter, is it even certain that he had much of an inheritance to squander. The story may nonetheless be substantially true, but as Chambers gives us no clue to its source, we have no way of judging its reliability for ourselves.

The real George Ormiston, who was born in 1672, probably succeeded his father without formality, as there is no mention of his appointment in the Town Council Minutes. His occupation is, at any rate, given as 'lockman' in the record of his first marriage, which took place in the Parish of Edinburgh on 15 July 1692.

By courtesy of Edinburgh City Libraries

The Hangman's Craig (the cliff in the centre of the picture): a photograph taken about 1900.

Edinburgh, August 15. The Magistrates of this City have been reprimanded by the Privy Council, for not seeing the Sentence upon the 4 Men concerned in the late Tumult, put in Execution, they having met with such Usage in their designed Punishment, as may rather encourage them to do the like in time to come, than deter them from it.

The Flying Post, 20-22 August 1700.

So he could only have been twenty at most when he was appointed, and was probably no more than sixteen. No other hangman is known to have held office at such a young age anywhere in Britain.

George's first wife, Jean Mason, bore him two daughters, Margaret and Marion, both of whom died in infancy: Margaret in 1693 and Marion in 1695. She then died herself in 1696, her burial taking place on 14 June of that year.

According to *The Ormistons of Teviotdale*, George then married Anna Coudoun, who bore him another daughter, Jean, in 1697. This union, however, seems not to have been a formal marriage, for on 18 September 1698, George was married to a Marion Lightbodie, who bore him a fourth child, Marie, in 1699. Both Jean and Marie also died young, though not in infancy.

George Ormiston remained hangman of Edinburgh until 1700, when an unusual sequence of events led to his dismissal. The affair began in June of that year, when an anti-English mob overran the city and attacked the homes of members and supporters of the Government. Some of the rioters burst into the Edinburgh Tolbooth and set free two men who had been apprehended for publishing inflammatory literature.

When order was restored, a number of arrests were made and the two men who had been released by the mob gave themselves up to the authorities. At the end of July, four young men were convicted of taking part in the disturbance: one of them, a cook named Charles Weir, was sentenced to be whipped, to stand in the pillory for one hour, and then to be banished from the kingdom. The others were sentenced to stand on the pillory with him; two of them were also to be banished from the city.

But the four men had the populace on their side, and when they were taken out to the pillory on 7 August, a large crowd cheered them on their way. Some of their supporters showered the pillory with flowers; others gave the offenders wine, much of which they consumed there and then. After the four men had stood on the pillory for an hour, Charles Weir was whipped by the hangman in a very lenient manner: one account states that the whipping was inflicted 'most gently'.

The Provost and bailies were outraged by Ormiston's conduct. They refused to accept his plea that he had been threatened with death if he 'laid on but one sore stroke', and ordered that he be whipped himself for failing to perform his duty. Ormiston was then put in prison while the Haddington hangman was sent for to administer this punishment.

The Haddington functionary duly arrived in Edinburgh, but the attitude of the crowds thronging the streets alarmed him and he fled. The whipping was apparently never carried out.

The following week it was reported that seven or eight servants of the Thistle Tavern, where Charles Weir was employed, had been imprisoned for bribing Ormiston to spare their fellow servant. Two days after that, the Provost and bailies were themselves reprimanded by the Privy Council for failing to ensure that the sentences imposed by the Criminal Court were properly executed.

Although he seems not to have been whipped, Ormiston *was* removed from office, his place being taken by a John Stewart, whose appointment is recorded in the Town Council Minutes for 30 August.

It is not known how long he was kept in jail or how he made his living after being released. Having been a public executioner for the whole of his adult life, he probably had difficulty finding even the most menial work. But he somehow managed to survive and was later reinstated as hangman. His reinstatement is recorded in the Council Minutes for 20 August 1701 as follows:

> The Councill being informed that ( ) Stewart present lockman had fled this Citie though he knew that one John Carss was to be executed(,) They therfore simpliciter depryve him of his office And ordaines the toun officers to search for him and apprehend and secure him into the Thieves Hole And in like manner the Councill does repone George Ormistoun late lockman to his office(.)

This time, however, Ormiston did not hold the post for long, for the following year he died. He was only about thirty years old at the time, but the circumstances of his death have not come to light.

The Town Council Minutes show that on 1 July 1702 a John Robertson was appointed to succeed him.

An anonymous work, *A Description of the Parish of Melrose*, published in Edinburgh in 1743, mentions George Ormiston in a paragraph about the possessions of the Ormiston family in the Melrose area of Roxburghshire, saying: 'It is said, that George Ormiston(,) late Hangman in Edinburgh, was a Cadet of this Family, if not the Representative of it; a Memorandum to old Families not to be puff'd up with Pride on account of their Antiquity, for they know not what mean Offices they or theirs may be obliged to stoop to.'

5. The Sailor, the Blacksmith and the Bailiff's Follower

In June 1706, the London hangman, Richard Pearse, petitioned the City's Court of Aldermen, begging for financial assistance. He was, he said, a very poor man, with nothing to maintain himself, and was fit for no other employment. He prayed that the Court, out of charity, would grant him something to keep him from starving.

Clearly, there was little work for him at the time, so the number of London and Middlesex hangings must have fallen to an unusually low level, possibly accompanied by a similar reduction in the number of lesser punishments he had to inflict. Yet the aldermen seem not to have regarded him as a deserving case, for they gave him nothing.

Pearse is the only London hangman from the period 1686-1714 of whom anything is known: even the names of the others are unrecorded. And nothing is known of Pearse himself except that he petitioned for relief on that one occasion without success. The next known occupant of the post was John Price, about whom we know quite a lot more.

Price, a native of London, was born about 1677. As a boy, he was apprenticed to a rag merchant, with whom he stayed until his master's death two years later; he then ran away and found work as a casual labourer. Eventually, he went to sea, and over the course of the next eighteen years served aboard several different men of war. It was after leaving the sea about the year 1714 that he obtained the post of hangman of London.

There must, by this time, have been a lot more hangings in London than there had been eight years earlier, for the office was now said to be worth about £40 a year when fees, gratuities and other perquisites were taken into account. Even so, Price lived beyond his means, and this led to his downfall.

One day in 1715, after carrying out a triple execution at Tyburn, he was arrested for a debt of 7s 6d. He managed to clear the debt and pay his creditor's costs, partly with money which he had in his possession and partly with the clothes of the offenders he had just hanged. But not long afterwards he was arrested for two further debts, and these he was unable to settle. So this time he was thrown into the Marshalsea Prison.

As a result of this confinement, Price was unable to perform his duties as hangman. He was therefore removed from the post and a new Jack Ketch appointed to take his place.

To Price, this was a terrible blow, leaving him with little chance of ever raising enough money to pay his debts. And, as luck would have it, it happened just as his prospects had been about to improve significantly following the collapse of that year's Jacobite rebellion.

*   *   *

William Marvell, the man who replaced Price as hangman, was a blacksmith by trade. He may also have been a pardoned capital offender.

A contemporary author, Captain Alexander Smith, mentions Marvell in his *Lives and Adventures of the most noted Bayliffs* (1723), claiming that the new hangman had twice been sentenced to death for theft by 1706. Although Smith's works are highly unreliable as sources of information, the printed *Old Bailey Sessions Papers* for 7-9 December 1709 contain the following entry:

> William Marvel alias Marven, of the Parish of St. Magnus, was Indicted for privately stealing 20 Yards of Muslin, value 4l. the Goods of Jeremy Shadwell, on the 17th of October last. It appear'd that the Prisoner came to the Prosecutor's Shop to buy Linnen, and the Prosecutor's back being turned to reach some, the Prisoner made use of that opportunity to take the Goods from the Counter, which were immediately found upon him. He being an old Offender, the Jury found him Guilty of the Indictment.

The offender in question was sentenced to death, but was not hanged and was pardoned a year later (as the *Sessions Papers* also show). There is no proof that the William Marvell who was appointed hangman in 1715 was the same person, but in view of what subsequently became of him, this *is* a distinct possibility.

Pardoned offender or not, Marvell the former blacksmith seems to have embarked on his new career as enthusiastically as any other member of the profession. In November 1715, in the Press Yard of Newgate Prison, he was seen celebrating the defeat of the Jacobite forces at Preston, in company with two members of the prison staff: an underling to one of the turnkeys and a deputy bedmaker, according to the person who recorded the event. He apparently believed that many of the rebels would be executed and that he personally stood to make a fortune out of their deaths.

In fact, only a small number of executions took place as a result of that rebellion, the most notable of them being those of the Earl of Derwentwater and Lord Kenmure. These rebel lords were both beheaded on Tower Hill on 24 February 1716, Kenmure giving the executioner a gratuity of eight guineas and Derwentwater probably giving him a similar sum. In all, the fees and gratuities which Marvell received in respect of these and other executions for treason during his first year in office obviously fell a long way short of a fortune, but must nonetheless have boosted his income to more than double what it would otherwise have been.

On 9 March 1716, just a fortnight after the execution of the rebel lords, the *Weekly-Journal or Saturday's-Post* reported that the hangman was 'dangerously ill of a consumption'. But eleven people were hanged at Tyburn three days later, and there is no evidence to suggest that anyone other than Marvell was their executioner. So presumably the report of his illness was based on a false rumour.

The following year, the *Original Weekly Journal* of 24-31 August reported in a far from respectful manner that Marvell was dead:

> We hear that on Sunday last John Ketch, alias Marvell, Esq; Executioner-General of the County of Middlesex, Departed this Life at his House in Broad St. Giles's, universally Regreted as well in regard of his Natural Experience and great Abilities in the due Performance of the several Parts of his Office, as for his agreeable Conversation.

The report went on to claim that the hangman had been married twice; that he had had three sons by his first wife, two of whom had been hanged and the third sentenced to transportation, and that he himself had been 'Door-keeper to the Bear-Garden' - 'which Office he discharg'd with great Fidelity and Applause' - some years earlier. It said nothing about his having been a blacksmith.

The report concluded by saying:

> The Corps of this great Person will be Interr'd some time next Week near Paddington, amongst those of his Ancestors. Who will succeed him in this Important Trust, is yet unknown; but there are already 14 Candidates for it, among whom we hear are three Thief takers, two Disbanded Footmen, a broken Change broker, and two Prize-fighters.

None of the claims made in this 'obituary' are corroborated by any other contemporary source and it is unlikely that any of them are true. It is also worthy of note that when Marvell was found not to be dead at all, the publisher of the *Original Weekly Journal* saw no need to announce the fact.

*   *   *

Just over two months after the publication of that report, Marvell was involved in an incident which led to his dismissal. It took place on the morning of 6 November 1717, while he was on his way to Tyburn to carry out a triple hanging.

Tyburn, it should be pointed out, was situated near the present-day Marble Arch, about two miles from Newgate Prison. On hanging days, spectators lined the streets to watch the condemned going by in carts, while others waited at the gallows, to make sure they had places from which they could see the executions.

On this occasion, the crowds were probably not very large, for it was a cold day and the condemned were not particularly well known. The hangman set out ahead of the procession on foot, unaware of the danger which lay before him.

After the unusually high earnings of his first year in office, Marvell's income had been greatly reduced in his second year, and, like his predecessor, he had fallen into debt. Now, as he made his way through the streets towards Tyburn, the former blacksmith was suddenly arrested by three bailiffs, who began to carry him off to jail. By a remarkable coincidence, this happened in Holborn, where John Price had been arrested two years earlier.

Marvell, however, was not taken far, for he somehow got the bailiffs to let him go. Perhaps he was able to settle his debts there and then; perhaps he just promised to settle them after the executions had been carried out. At any rate, he was released by the bailiffs, but fell into the hands of an unruly mob almost immediately afterwards. The mob, probably recognizing him as the hangman, attacked and beat him unmercifully, so that by the time they had finished with him he was quite incapable of resuming his journey.

The procession thus reached Tyburn with three men in the hanging-cart and nobody to hang them. The Under-Sheriff, who was in charge of the proceedings, had therefore to try to find somebody else to officiate in Marvell's place. A bricklayer showed a willingness to do so, but other spectators, having by now made up their minds to prevent justice from taking its course, began threatening him with violence. He then gave up the idea.

After that, nobody would volunteer, and after being kept waiting in the cold for two hours, the condemned men were taken back to Newgate. In view of what had happened, they were initially reprieved and then pardoned on condition of being transported to America. One of them, a burglar named John Meff, was, however, hanged four years later for returning from transportation before his seven-year term had expired.

A few days after being beaten up (and, according to one account, ducked in a horse-pond), Marvell was removed from office for allegedly neglecting his duty. A man named Banks, described as a bailiff's follower, was appointed hangman in his place.

On 30 November, the *Weekly-Journal or Saturday's-Post* reported in a derisive fashion that 'the Right Worshipful John Ketch Esq' was 'in a fair way of recovering his Post of Honour'. The report continued:

> It seems his Worship had petitioned the Sheriffs of London and Middlesex to be restored, and being resolved to speak handsomly to his Cause, dress'd himself up in the Trophies of his Office Vest, the fine Linnen, and embroider'd Wastcoat of two honest Gentlemen, that had pass'd under his Operation, over which he put a very handsom (BORROW'D) Coat, and so appeared in a Figure suitable to the Dignity of his Personal Employment.

Whether there was any truth in this story, it is impossible to ascertain. But if there was, then Marvell's attempt to impress the sheriffs was to no avail, for they did not reinstate him. He had done all the hanging he was ever going to do.

The following week, the new hangman was called upon to inflict a form of judicial torture on three soldiers who had been arraigned for felony at the Old Bailey but refused to plead to the charges against them.

Under English law at this time, a trial for felony could not begin until the accused had pleaded to the indictment, and some prisoners tried to avoid conviction by not doing so. In such cases, the accused was usually subjected to the frightful ordeal of *peine forte et dure*.

The infliction of this revolting punishment would take place in some prison room or dungeon, where the prisoner, wearing just a loincloth, would be stretched out on his back and would have heavy weights placed on his chest until he was crushed to death or begged to be allowed to stand trial.*

An alternative means of forcing prisoners to plead which was sometimes used at the Old Bailey in the early eighteenth century was to have their thumbs tied together with whipcord, as if for the ritual of condemnation (see p.1) and the ends of the cord pulled hard. It was this procedure which was followed in the case of the three soldiers, who then agreed to stand trial and were all convicted.

*   *   *

John Price remained in the Marshalsea for many months, but eventually he and another prisoner escaped through a hole in the wall. He was then at liberty until early in 1718, when he committed a brutal murder.

On the night of 13 March of that year, Price was apprehended by two other men after attacking a woman in Bunhill Fields. The two men had caught him trying to rape Mrs Elizabeth White, the wife of a watchman, as she lay seriously injured on the ground, and had carried him off to a watchhouse, covered in blood.

Mrs White, who sold cakes and gingerbread in the streets, had been savagely beaten. One of her eyes had been knocked out of its socket, her scalp was badly bruised, her throat was bruised; she also had a broken arm and a lacerated womb. She died of her injuries four days later, having been unable to speak in the meantime.

Price was held overnight in the watchhouse, then taken before a justice and committed to Newgate. On 23 April, he appeared at the Old Bailey, to stand trial for Mrs White's murder. He denied the crime, but could have had little real hope

---

* Legally, *peine forte et dure* was a form of execution and sentence of death was passed on the prisoner before he was subjected to it. By the eighteenth century, however, he was generally allowed, as a favour, to halt the proceedings by asking to be allowed to stand trial. It was the trial judge who decided whether the favour should be granted.

An inaccurate portrayal of William Marvell's encounter with the bailiffs, showing him in the hanging-cart at the time. He had actually gone on ahead of it on foot. (From *The Malefactor's Register.*)

A prisoner undergoing *peine forte et dure*, or pressing to death (from *The Malefactor's Register*).

On Wednesday the Sessions began at the Old-Baily, where a Dutchman, who was Valet de Chambre to a German Gentleman was try'd for the murdering his Master the 8th of October, and flinging his Body into a Pond near St. Giles's, and found guilty. Three Soldiers, who some Time ago robb'd some Higglers coming to Town, near Acton, were brought to the Bar and would not plead to their Indictment; upon which the new Hangman ty'd up their Thumbs so hard that they agreed to plead rather than be carried to Newgate to be pressed (to) Death, which the Court granted; and after full Proof in their Tryal, the Jury brought them in guilty.

The Weekly-Journal or Saturday's-Post, 7 December 1717.

of being acquitted.

The two eyewitnesses both told the court that they had found the prisoner lying on the ground with the deceased. One said that he was 'busy about her', the other that the woman's clothes were up to her belly.

Both men said that when they arrived on the scene Price had said to them, 'Damn you! What do you want?' Both also said that when asked what he was doing, the prisoner had replied that his victim was 'nothing but a drunken woman'.

Price claimed that on the night in question he had been crossing Bunhill Fields when he found the woman lying in his way. He said he lifted her up but found that she was unable to stand, and that it was then that he was apprehended. The story was quite unconvincing.

Reporting his conviction, the *Weekly-Journal or Saturday's-Post* of 26 April said that Price was 'such a harden'd Villain that he appeared not at all concerned' about it. The report added that he 'went afterwards upon the Leads, and took the present Hangman by the Hand, telling him he hang'd a great many, and now he must hang him'. It is unclear whether the leads referred to were at the courthouse or at Newgate Prison.

Following condemnation, Price spent another five weeks in Newgate, presumably in the Condemned Hold. This was a dark ground-floor cell, about twenty feet by fourteen, where male prisoners under sentence of death were kept in irons until they were either hanged or pardoned.

The room had stone walls, a heavy door with a row of spikes along the top of it and an open sewer running through the middle of the floor. The floor also had boarded-over areas where the condemned slept and hooks, iron staples and chains to which they could be secured if they became unruly.*

---

* Wealthy prisoners generally paid to have their own rooms, with members of the prison staff to wait on them.

The hanging of John Price at the scene of his crime (an illustration from *The Sorrowful Lamentation*, a contemporary ballad).

While awaiting execution, Price continued to deny the crime for which he had been sentenced. On the day he was hanged, the *Weekly-Journal or Saturday's-Post* reported that 'he hath since Sentence of Condemnation been drunk for several Days successively, and committed most horrid outrages'. There was no indication of what these 'horrid outrages' might have been, but a fortnight later, the *Original Weekly Journal* claimed:

A Little Girl who used to carry Victuals to John Price the Hangman in Newgate, has declared that a few Days before his Execution, he had Carnal Knowledge of her Body in the said (Gaol).

Price was hanged on 31 May 1718, not at Tyburn but on a temporary gallows at the scene of his crime: a fate reserved for murderers of the worst type. At the place of execution, he finally confessed his guilt, saying that he had been 'much in liquor' when the crime was committed. He then joined the Ordinary of Newgate (the prison chaplain) in prayer and the Ordinary, at his request, urged the spectators to take warning from his untimely end.

That afternoon, Price's body was gibbeted at Stonebridge, near Holloway. The suit of iron in which it was hung had been made by William Marvell, who, since his own dismissal from the post of hangman, had gone back to working as a blacksmith.

John Price, an illiterate man, was forty-one years old at the time of his death. It appears from one account of his execution that he still called himself 'the finisher of the law', even though he had held no such post for three years.

A contemporary ballad, *The Sorrowful Lamentation and last Farewel of John Price, alias Jack Ketch,* suggests that he was a bigamist several times over. But there is no hint of this in the newspapers of the time and the reports of his trial and execution do not tell us whether he was married at all. It does, however, seem that he *was* married and that his wife only outlived him by two years, for in the *Weekly-Journal or Saturday's-Post* of 28 May 1720 we find the following report:

> In the same Prison (Newgate) died one Price, Widow of the late Hangman, who, had she lived, was to have been transported.

Unfortunately, no further details of the case were ever published, as far as we know.

* * *

The year after Price was hanged, Marvell was accused of theft - perhaps not for the first time.

The affair began on 7 August 1719, when he entered a haberdasher's shop in Coleman Street, wearing an apron and carrying a lock under his arm. He argued about the price of some handkerchiefs, then took one of them to show to a woman who was standing at the door. After he had left the shop, ten other handkerchiefs (all silk) were found to be missing from the counter.

The shopkeeper's daughter ran out into the street to look for the culprit, but by this time there was no sign of him anywhere. He had, however, been seen and recognized by a woman standing outside a nearby alehouse, but, even so, it was not until six weeks later that he was apprehended.

When he was finally confronted with the haberdasher's wife and daughter, Marvell admitted stealing the handkerchiefs, which were together valued at twelve shillings. He said he had been drunk at the time and offered to pay for them if the shopkeeper would accept a shilling a week, but the offer was refused.

Marvell was then taken before a justice and committed for trial. On arrival at Newgate Prison, he was unruly and so was put into the Condemned Hold.

On 15 October, he appeared for trial at the Old Bailey, charged with stealing the ten handkerchiefs. He pleaded not guilty. From the *Sessions Papers*, it seems that the haberdasher's wife and daughter were both positive that Marvell was the man who had been in the shop when the handkerchiefs disappeared; that they were equally sure that the handkerchiefs had been on the counter when he entered and that nobody else had come in before they were missed. The *Sessions Papers* also inform us that the evidence of these witnesses was corroborated by a third woman who had been in the shop all the time the prisoner was there.

'The Prisoner owned his being in the Shop to buy a Handkerchief, but denied that he took any away, and said that he was prosecuted out of Malice, several having bore him an Ill Will for performing his Office in cutting off the Earl of Derwentwater's Head,' this record of the proceedings continues.

> He called several who gave him the Character of an Honest and Industrious Man, and some of them added, that they had heard him declare he resolved to continue so as long as he lived, and that he would rather beg than steal; for that if he should be taken in Stealing but one penny, his very Character would hang him; that he did sometimes beg and they had relieved him.

Marvell was on trial for his life, for it was a capital offence at this time to steal

Convicts under sentence of transportation in the early eighteenth century on their way from Newgate to Blackfriars Stairs, to begin the journey to America (from an old print).

from a shop to the value of five shillings. But the jury, though convinced by the evidence produced against him, were unwilling to send him to the gallows. They therefore undervalued the goods that had been stolen and brought him in guilty only of stealing to the value of 4s 10d. This was an expedient which was often used by juries in such cases - sometimes they even undervalued coins and banknotes - in order to ensure that the prisoner was not hanged.

The erstwhile Jack Ketch was therefore sentenced to transportation. The *Sessions Papers* do not give the length of his term (it was probably seven years) but say that 'he beg'd of the Court not to send him beyond Sea; but to admit him to any Corporal Punishment they should think fit, which he would willingly submit to, tho' it were to be Whipt a Mile'. The plea failed to secure any further mitigation of punishment.

A week later, on 23 October 1719, a party of convicts - eighty of them according to one newspaper, ninety-one according to another - left Newgate between five and six o'clock in the morning and were conveyed down the Thames from Blackfriars Stairs to Woolwich. Marvell was among them.

At Woolwich, they were put aboard a transport ship bound for the tobacco-producing colony of Maryland, where those who survived the journey were to serve their sentences in conditions of virtual slavery.

In its report of the convicts' departure, the *Original Weekly Journal* informed its readers of Marvell's plea to be whipped rather than transported. It concluded mockingly that 'tho' his Request was not fully answer'd, as to his earnest Desire of being whip'd at home, yet, in some Measure, it was granted, at his going abroad, for they whip'd him away on board, among the rest of his Brethren in Iniquity'.

This was the last that was ever heard of Marvell in England, and his name does not appear in the landing certificate issued at the ship's port of arrival. It would therefore seem that, like many other prisoners sentenced to transportation in the early eighteenth century, he died on the voyage across the Atlantic.

6. 'Dick Arnold' and the Comical Fellow

Banks did not remain hangman of London for long. It is not known what became of him, but his successor was already in office by the early part of 1719.

Richard Arnet, who seems generally to have been called Richard or Dick Arnold, is mentioned in Captain Alexander Smith's *Life and Times of Jonathan Wild* (1726), in connection with a multiple hanging carried out at Tyburn on 13 February 1719. His name also appears in a tract, *A Seasonable Hue and Cry after the Pretender*, published the following month. But neither of these sources give any indication of how long he had been in office, so his appointment may actually have taken place several months earlier.

Arnet, at any rate, was the London functionary by March 1719 at the latest, and it is also known that he was still in office at his death in 1728. He must therefore have held the post for at least nine years, during which hundreds of offenders were hanged at Tyburn. Unfortunately, little is known about him personally, for he did not get into any trouble himself and the journalists of the time did not find him newsworthy.

An early incident in Arnet's career was the whipping of a chairman named Moor from Somerset House to the Haymarket for insulting a member of the Royal Family. This took place on 16 April 1719, and was witnessed by a large number of people.

According to a report in the *Weekly Journal or British Gazetteer*, the hangman 'follow'd his Work pretty close' and made the culprit cry, 'God bless King George!' before he had finished with him. This pleased the spectators, many of whom 'carress'd and applauded the Executioner after his Work was over'.

Arnet's salary, at his death, is known to have been £20 a year. But, like previous holders of the post, he also had a variety of fees, gratuities and other perquisites. One of his perquisites was a regular Christmas box from the Company of Barber-Surgeons.

The Company, at this time, had great difficulty obtaining corpses to use as subjects for dissection. A few times each year it would be authorized to take the body of some executed criminal for this purpose, but the practice of anatomiz-ation was popularly abhorred and the Company's beadles were often obstructed by the crowds. The hangman was thus given a Christmas box every year (2s 6d in 1717, 7s 6d in 1730), in order to ensure his co-operation. On one occasion, in 1720, the Company even compensated him for the loss of a hanged man's clothes during a scuffle.

The London hangman's right to the clothes of his victims was a valuable source of income, for some offenders dressed well for their executions. But others deliberately wore clothes of poor quality rather than allow their best garments to fall into his hands. During Arnet's tenure of office, some even went to the gallows wearing their burial shrouds, to make sure that the hangman got none of their clothes at all.

One person who did this was Stephen Gardener, a highwayman and house-breaker hanged in 1724; on another occasion, a year later, *three* condemned prisoners (out of a total of eight) went to the gallows similarly attired. In this second case, which took place on 30 April 1725, one of the people concerned apparently tried to escape, for *Mist's Weekly Journal* reported:

> The two Foot-Pads and Swaffo's Man, went to Tyburn in their Shrowds; and the latter, when they were going to be ty'd up, slipp'd his Head out of the Halter, leap'd out of the Cart among the Mob, and began to tear off his Shrowd; but his Hands were ty'd, and he could do but little at it: Jack Ketch leap'd upon his Back, and the Sheriffs Officers surrounded him, so that he was soon taken, re-halter'd, and hang'd.

Among the many other offenders who suffered at Arnet's hands was William Spiggott, a highwayman who 'stood mute' when he appeared for trial in January 1721. In this case, the tying of the prisoner's thumbs proved unavailing and he was sentenced to be pressed to death.

Spiggott endured weights totalling 350 lb on his chest for half an hour, but when a further 50 lb was added he begged to be taken back to court to plead. He was then tried and convicted, and on 8 February he was hanged at Tyburn with three other men.

Towards the end of the same year, another highwayman, Nathaniel Hawes, stood mute in the same courthouse. He, too, was pressed (the tying of *his* thumbs having also proved ineffectual), but gave up after bearing 250 lb for about seven minutes. He was hanged on 22 December.

Three years later, on 16 November 1724, Arnet hanged Jack Sheppard, a young housebreaker and jailbreaker who had made two remarkable escapes from Newgate while under sentence of death. Sheppard was a popular hero and his execution attracted an enormous crowd of people. Fears that his body was to be dissected sparked off a riot, which did not subside until troops were called out to deal with it.

Many of the people hanged by Arnet in his first six years in office were victims of the thief-taker Jonathan Wild, who apprehended scores of highway-men, housebreakers and other offenders while at the same time running a criminal empire of his own. Wild was himself hanged on 24 May 1725 for selling a quantity of stolen lace back to its rightful owner.

Wild was a much-hated figure and the crowd which turned out for his

The hanging of Stephen Gardener, who went to the gallows wearing his burial shroud (from *The Newgate Calendar*, 1773).

execution was even bigger than the one which had attended Sheppard's. On the way to the gallows, he was pelted with stones and suffered head injuries; two highwaymen who were to be hanged with him were also hurt.

At the Triple Tree, Wild went on sitting in the cart after the two highwaymen and a third prisoner, a coiner, had been tied up, the executioner having told him that he could have 'any reasonable time' in which to prepare himself. But the regular Tyburn mob was impatient to see him suffer and threatened to knock the hangman on the head if he did not perform his duty immediately. Fearing for his own safety, Arnet then gave way to their demands.

On 11 June the same year, a multiple execution was carried out at Execution Dock in Wapping. This was the traditional place of execution for offenders whose crimes had been committed at sea. The hangings were carried out on the foreshore at low tide, and in cases of piracy the culprits' bodies were afterwards gibbeted on the riverbank.

Multiple executions at this site were by no means uncommon: the largest ever carried out there was probably one which took place in 1700, when twenty-four pirates were hanged together. At the one which took place in June 1725, nine pirates were hanged, two of whom were so weak that they had to be carried from the hanging-carts on men's backs.

On 9 May the following year, a woman named Catherine Hayes was burnt at the stake at Tyburn for the murder of her husband. With two male accomplices, she had battered the victim to death and dismembered his body in an attempt to conceal the crime. The three culprits were all sentenced to death, but one of the men, Thomas Wood, died in prison while awaiting execution. The other, Thomas Billings, was hanged and gibbeted.

In cases in which a woman was convicted of treason (which included coining) or petty treason (the murder of her husband) the penalty was death by burning. In practice, the condemned was usually afforded the favour of being strangled before she was burnt, and for this purpose a halter would be placed round her neck and the rope passed through a hole in the stake. After the faggots had been lit, the hangman would pull the free end of the rope, strangling the condemned before the flames reached her.

In Catherine Hayes's case, however, the flames spread faster than he had expected and burnt his hand. This caused him to let go of the rope, with the result that Mrs Hayes was inadvertently burnt alive.

Despite this ghastly accident, Arnet was allowed to retain his post, and so went on carrying out his frightful duties for another two years. Finally, in August 1728, he died and was succeeded as hangman by a man named John Hooper. The *Weekly Journal or British Gazetteer* of Saturday, 17 August recorded Arnet's funeral and Hooper's appointment as follows:

The burning of Catherine Hayes for the murder of her husband
(from the Rev John Villette's *Annals of Newgate*, 1776).

On Tuesday Night the Body of Mr. Richard Arnold the Hangman, was convey'd from his House in Deptford to the Parish Church there to be interred: The Chief Mourners were Little Tom his truly lamenting Servant, and his Wife, &c. Capt. John Hooper is made Hangman in the Room of the said Richard Arnold, being a Person of known Probity and Integrity, and who merits the Place by his unspotted Character.

The Burial Register of St Nicholas's Church, Deptford Green, confirms that 'Richd. Arnet' *was* buried there, and gives the date of his interment as 14 August.

*   *   *

'Captain' John Hooper, as he was called in at least two newspapers, was not a captain at all: nor was he a dealer in pack-thread, as the *Gloucester Journal* claimed. He was actually an assistant to one of the turnkeys at Newgate.

He had evidently been employed at the prison in one capacity or another for some time, for over a year earlier he had been given the special duty of acting as personal jailer to Major John Oneby, a privileged prisoner who had killed another man during a quarrel. An account of the Oneby case in the anonymous *Select Trials at the Sessions-House in the Old-Bailey* (1742) tells us quite a lot about Hooper's personality:

> The Person appointed to lie a Nights in the Major's Room was John Hooper, the present Executioner, who was one thought well qualified for so important a Trust. And indeed his Behaviour answered the Character given him, for he acquitted himself so well in this Employment, that, the Place of Executioner being afterwards vacant, he was immediately promoted to it by Virtue of his own personal Merit, without Bribery or Corruption.
>
> But as honest a Fellow as Jack was, yet, when the Keeper introduced him to the Major, the Major it seems did not much like his Looks; for, says he, What the Devil do ye bring this Fellow here for? whenever I look at him I shall think of hanging.
>
> A few Days, however, not only reconciled the Major to his new Companion, but made him even fond of his Company, for Jack was a comical Fellow: He would tell a hundred wild, out-of-the-way Stories, writhe his Face to all the Figures in Geometry, preach Sermons, say his Prayers, and play a World of Monkey Tricks, with which the Major was mightily diverted.

On 3 July 1727, Oneby committed suicide in order to avoid the gallows. In a brief will, he left half a guinea to one of the turnkeys and five shillings to Hooper, explaining, 'The poor Devils have had a great deal of Trouble with me since I have been here.'

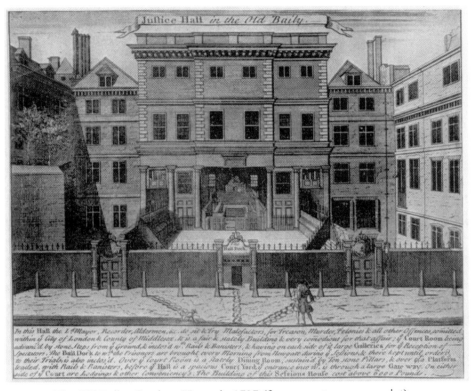

The Old Bailey Sessions House in 1727 (from a contemporary print).

Ten months later, Hooper was attacked while escorting a female prisoner back to Newgate from the Old Bailey, where she had just been convicted of a capital offence. His assailant, described in one newspaper as 'a lusty Fellow, with a great Oaken Stick', struck the assistant turnkey on the head in an attempt to rescue the prisoner, Mary Jenkins. Hooper, however, managed to prevent the prisoner from escaping and his attacker was apprehended a few days later.

Hooper's appointment as hangman of London and Middlesex took place on 15 August 1728, just one day after Richard Arnet's funeral. Eight days later, he carried out his first execution: that of James Haddock, who was hanged at Tyburn for stealing goods from his lodgings in Hammersmith.

Like Arnet, Hooper went on to hold the post for several years, though he was not still in office in 1742, as the *Select Trials* extract suggests. He had died or left office by March 1735.

The *Select Trials* portrayal of Hooper as a 'comical fellow' led Horace Bleackley, the author of *The Hangmen of England* (1929), to assume that

Wednesday the 13 following Malefactors were executed at Tyburn, viz John Brown, Henry Bagster, John Rooke, William Brown, Joseph Whitlock, William Johnson, John Anderson, Francis Ogleby, James Baker, alias Stick in the Mud, Thomas Whitby, John Collington, Elizabeth Wright, and John Beach.

John Brown and Elizabeth Wright, for Coining, were drawn on a Sledge by four Horses to the Place of Execution, and were very penitent, and the latter, (pursuant to her Sentence) was tyed to a Stake and burnt to Ashes.

John Beach, who was executed for a Street Robbery, when he was taken out of the Cells at Newgate, denied the Fact for which he suffered, and when he was in the Cart, declared he would not be hang'd in his Shoes, and so took them off and threw them amongst the Mob.

The Country Journal or the Craftsman, 22 December 1733.

'laughing Jack' regularly cheered the condemned at the place of execution. But we have no evidence that he ever did this and it may be seriously doubted whether he would have been allowed to behave in such a manner while they were being prepared for their final ordeals. The idea just doesn't seem credible.

It is, however, of interest to note that *The Hangmen of England* also contains a reproduction of a sample of Hooper's handwriting. It is only his signature, followed by the word *Executioner,* but it is sufficient to show that he was literate. It is reproduced from a receipt book kept by the Company of Barber-Surgeons.

Hooper, like his predecessor, officiated at Tyburn several times a year. The hangings he carried out were generally multiple ones: on 11 November 1728, for example, thirteen people were hanged together; the same number were hanged on 9 October 1732. On 29 January 1733, twelve were hanged; on 19 December the same year there were twelve again. There were also a number of burnings at Tyburn during the years that Hooper held office.

Besides all the executions, he had many whippings to inflict. Usually they were carried out in public, at the cart's tail, but some were apparently 'private' whippings. 'Yesterday 7 Night Katherine Pember was whipp'd in Newgate by the Hangman, and then discharg'd,' says the *British Journal* of 21 February 1730.

In 1731, Hooper carried out a revolting sentence of pillorying and mutilation on a man named Japhet Crooke, who had been convicted of forging deeds of conveyance of a piece of land at Clacton-on-Sea, Essex. The pillorying and mutilation, which were only part of his punishment (he was also to be imprisoned for life), were carried out on 10 June of that year and were described in detail in the *Daily Courant* the following day.

The *Courant* said that the culprit was brought by the Keeper of the King's Bench (that being the prison where he had been confined) to Charing Cross, 'where he stood on the Pillory from Twelve to One, pursuant to his Sentence'. The account then went on to say that

> the Time being near expired, he was set on a Chair on the Pillory, when the Hangman, dress'd like a Butcher came to him, attended by two Surgeons, and with a Knife, made like a Gardiner's Pruning Knife, cut off both his Ears, and with a Pair of Scissers slit both his Nostrils, which were afterwards sear'd with a hot Iron; all which he bore most surprizingly, till his Nostrils were burnt, which put him to great Torture(.)

Afterwards, according to the *Courant*, the offender was carried to a nearby tavern, where his wounds were dressed, then taken back to the King's Bench, where his prison sentence was to be served.

Another report of the spectacle, published in the *Country Journal or the Craftsman*, said that only the culprit's right nostril was seared and that he left the pillory bleeding.

* * *

Of the many offenders executed by Hooper, the most celebrated was probably Sarah Malcolm, a young laundress and charwoman who killed her elderly employer, a Mrs Duncombe, and two fellow servants, in order to steal money and other valuables belonging to the former. The triple murder took place at Mrs Duncombe's home in the Temple early in 1733, and in view of the gravity of the crime, the condemned woman was hanged in Fleet Street, just a short distance from the scene.

'Wednesday Sarah Malcolm was executed before Mitre Court in Fleet Street, for the Murder of Mrs. Duncomb, &c. in the Temple,' reported the *Universal Spectator and Weekly Journal* of Saturday, 10 March 1733.

> She came to the Gibbet between Ten and Eleven o'Clock, and appeared very serious and devout, crying and wringing her Hands in an extraordinary Manner: She was assisted in her Devotions by the Rev. Mr. Peddington (of St Bartholomew's, Smithfield), and Mr. Guthrie (the Ordinary of Newgate) attended in the Cart. She declared to the People, that her Master knew nothing of her Intentions of the Robbery, &c. and said that she had given to Mr. Peddington a Letter, which related what she had to say to the Fact.

The account went on to say that while the culprit was in the cart 'she fell down; but immediately was rais'd, and laid her Head against Jack Ketch, and Mr. Peddington read to her'. At length, she was turned off and left hanging for about half an hour. She was then cut down, put into a coach and carried back to

Newgate.

Sarah Malcolm's execution attracted a great many spectators. *Read's Weekly Journal* of 10 March gives the following information about them:

> Several of the Nobility, and other Persons of Distinction, saw the Execution from the neighbouring Houses; and there was as great a Concourse of common People as ever was seen on the like Occasion. Many of the Spectators were hurt by the breaking down of a Scaffold; and very few of the Ladies and Gentlemen but had their Pockets either pick'd or cut off.

A few weeks after the hanging of Sarah Malcolm, a Mr Chevett or Chovet, a surgeon, tried to save the life of a condemned highwayman named William Gordon by inserting a silver tube in his windpipe before he was hanged and bleeding and warming him after he had been cut down. The attempt was unsuccessful.

Then, on 28 May the same year, there was another dramatic attempt to escape from the hanging-cart at the place of execution. This is how the *Gentleman's Magazine* described the incident:

> John Jones and Jn Davis, condemn'd for Robberies on the Highway, were executed at Tyburn. Davis feign'd himself sick, and desir'd he might not be ty'd in the Cart: But when he came to the Tree, while the Hangman was fastening the other's Halter, he jumpt out of the Cart, and ran over 2 Fields; but being knock'd down by a Countryman, was convey'd back and hang'd without any more Ceremony.

The last known newspaper report to mention Hooper by name was an item which appeared in the *Universal Spectator* of 31 March 1733. This informs us that on 26 March an issue of the *Daily Courant* was publicly burnt by him 'for containing false and scandalous Reflections on the Merchants and Traders of this City, for their Opposition to the Excise'. A search of many other newspapers of the time has failed to throw any light on what subsequently became of him.

The earliest indication of his having left office is to be found in the *Old Whig* newspaper of 13 March 1735, from which we learn that a new hangman had carried out a multiple execution at Tyburn three days earlier.

7. Another Hangman Convicted of Murder

The first known hangman of London after Hooper was a man named John Thrift, who was probably his immediate successor. There is no record of Thrift's appointment, but a report in the *General Evening Post* of 22-25 May 1736 shows that he was already in office by that time and gives no indication that he was new to it. It therefore seems likely (as Horace Bleackley assumed) that he was the new hangman who officiated at Tyburn on 10 March the previous year.

If so, then his conduct on his first hanging day resulted in a minor mishap. It was, by this time, customary at Tyburn (as it eventually became throughout the country) for white nightcaps to be placed on the heads of the condemned and pulled down over their faces just before they were 'launched into Eternity'. If no nightcaps were available, pieces of plain white cloth were used instead.

Hangings at Tyburn were carried out from the backs of carts, the condemned being turned off in batches of eight or less. As there were thirteen to be hanged on this occasion, two carts were used, one of which was drawn away before all of the offenders' caps were pulled down. The *Old Whig* described the mishap as follows:

> After the Ordinary had finished, and was gone out of the Cart, the Executioner was in such a Hurry, being the first Time of his performing the Office, that he drew away the Cart before all their Caps were pulled over their Faces, and so exposed them to the Multitude.

There is no suggestion in the report that the hangman got into any trouble over this mistake.

If Thrift *was* John Hooper's immediate successor, then his first year as hangman of London - a post which he was to hold until his death seventeen years later - was fairly uneventful. But in May 1736 he had the unpleasant experience of being committed to prison on a charge of robbery. It is a report of this incident which contains the earliest known reference to Thrift by name:

> Yesterday about Nine in the Evening was committed to Newgate by Justice Midford, John Thrift, otherwise call'd Jack Catch, on the Oath of Mary White, for assaulting and knocking down, and forcibly taking away from her, in his own House, a strip'd Ticken Pocket, in which were 3s. 6d. He was but just return'd from doing his Duty at Tyburn when he committed the above Robbery.

Thrift was not tried for the alleged crime, for after he had spent nearly a fortnight in jail, Mary White's accusation was found to be false. Thrift was then set free and his accuser committed to prison in his place. She, however, seems not to have been brought to trial for falsely accusing him and no further reports of the affair were published.

We do not know where Thrift lived at this time. In March 1750, he was living in Coal Yard, Drury Lane, an alley running parallel to High Holborn, but it is not known how long he had been there. Nor do we know whether Mary White was somebody of his acquaintance.

It is quite possible that she was a friend or relative of somebody he had hanged.

* * *

On the day that Mary White accused him of robbing her, Thrift had hanged four malefactors at Tyburn. The executions appear to have taken place without incident, but violence erupted afterwards, when one of the bodies was taken for dissection.

A mob wrested the body from the surgeons' beadles and fought with constables of the Holborn Division in their determination to keep possession of it. The constables managed to retake the body, but several of them were injured in the fighting, as were some of the rioters.

This was just one of many disorders which broke out at executions in London during Thrift's sixteen- or seventeen-year tenure of office. There was another one just two months later, when Thomas Reynolds, a turnpike leveller condemned under the Waltham Black Act of 1723, was found to be still alive after being cut down from the Triple Tree.

Reynolds had been put into his coffin, the lid of which was about to be fastened down when he suddenly thrust it back and started to get up. The *General Evening Post's* account of the execution says that the astonished crowd initially wanted the condemned man to be knocked on the head, but Thrift insisted that he be hanged again. At this, says the *Post*, 'the Mob taking a different turn, cry'd Save his Life, and fell upon the poor Executioner (who stickled hard for fulfilling the Law) and beat him in a most miserable Manner'.

Reynolds was carried off by the mob to a house in Acton, where he was put to bed but died after being given a glass of wine. Thrift, who had personally cut him down from the gallows, had not been alone in thinking the hanged man was dead. 'The Sheriffs Officers believing the Prisoner dead, were retir'd from the Place of Execution before he was cut down,' the *Post's* report concludes.

This was the only occasion on which Thrift is known to have been attacked at an execution. But hostile crowds must often have posed a threat to his safety and there may well have been other attacks on him that were not reported.

*   *   *

Other noteworthy hangings carried out by John Thrift include one which took place at Execution Dock in 1738. This was the abortive execution of James Buchanan, a Scottish seaman who had committed a murder aboard an English merchant ship lying at anchor in China's Canton River.

Buchanan was hanged on a temporary scaffold, as was usual at this place of execution, but while he was still alive a party of his fellow sailors forced their way onto it and cut him down. They then carried him to a boat which was waiting nearby and set off along the river towards Deptford. Buchanan was never recaptured, nor were any of his rescuers ever caught. It was a case unique in the annals of English crime.

In 1740, another culprit was found to be still alive after being hanged at Tyburn: this was William Duell, a youth of seventeen who had been convicted of rape. Duell was hanged with four other prisoners and was then cut down and taken to Surgeons' Hall. While he was being prepared for dissection, he was found to be breathing and one of the surgeons resuscitated him. Duell was afterwards pardoned on condition of being transported to America for life.*

In 1743, a man named Thomas Rounce was hanged, drawn and quartered at Execution Dock for fighting against his King and Country aboard a Spanish privateer.

Rounce was drawn from Newgate to Wapping on a hurdle pulled by four horses. 'Jack Ketch rode upon the Hurdle, dress'd in a white Frock, with a Knife and Steel by his Side, and a drawn Scymetar in his Hand,' says the *London Evening-Post* of 18-20 January.

At the place of execution, the condemned man was turned off and left hanging for about fifteen minutes, after which 'the Executioner cut him down, ript up his Belly, and threw his Heart and Bowels into a Fire prepar'd for that Purpose,' the *Evening-Post's* account continues. 'He was then quarter'd, and his Quarters put into a Coffin, and deliver'd to his Friends.'

The execution apparently caused much excitement, for the report concludes by saying, 'The Crowd was so great that several People had their Legs and Arms broke, and were otherwise terribly bruis'd.'

Following the Jacobite Rebellion of 1745, Thrift carried out further executions for treason. These included the hanging, drawing and quartering of nine men on Kennington Common on 30 July 1746, and the beheading of the rebel lords Kilmarnock and Balmerino on Tower Hill nineteen days later.

---

* There is a more detailed account of the case of James Buchanan in *Crime Strange But True* (Futura Publications, 1991), also by James Bland. *The Book of Executions* (Warner Books, 1993), by the same author, gives further details of William Duell's case and also those of three other offenders who were resuscitated after being hanged.

The hanging of a pirate at Execution Dock (from *The Male-factor's Register*).

The hanging, drawing and quartering of Jacobite rebels on
Kennington Common in 1746 (from *The Annals of Newgate*).
The quartering of the bodies began with decapitation.

The beheading of one of the rebel lords by John Thrift (from *The Annals of Newgate*).

On the latter occasion, Thrift lost his nerve on the scaffold and had to be fortified with wine before he could perform the first execution. He nonetheless managed to cut off Kilmarnock's head at the first attempt - but it then took him three strokes to cut off Balmerino's.

Lord Lovat, who was beheaded by Thrift on 9 April the following year, was the last person to suffer this form of execution in England. He was eighty years old.

* * *

Five years after he was maliciously prosecuted by Mary White, Thrift was reported to be in trouble with the law again. 'On Saturday last John Swift (*sic*), alias Jack Ketch, was committed by Justice Hervey to the Gatehouse for an Assault,' says the *Daily Gazetteer* of 26 January 1741. But no further details of the affair were reported, so this prosecution was obviously dropped.

Later the same year, Thrift was summoned to Surgeons' Hall to answer a complaint from the Company's beadles about his behaviour at an execution. He had apparently tried to prevent them from taking corpses to which their employers were entitled and had threatened to make further difficulties for them in future.

Thrift's appearance before the Company's Court of Assistants took place on 24 September, as we know from an entry in one of the Company's minute books. This shows that he was rebuked by the Court, and that the Court then decided to report the matter to the Lord Mayor and Court of Aldermen, 'in order to prevent his intended proceedings'. In spite of this, however, Thrift continued to receive Christmas boxes from the Surgeons, so it is unlikely that he gave them any further cause for complaint.

A little under two years later, the hangman gave evidence at the Old Bailey against a boy of twelve named Evan Evans, who stood charged with stealing three large silver spoons, three teaspoons and a salt-spoon just a day or two earlier. Thrift had himself had the boy apprehended after the boy allegedly tried to involve him in the crime. Evan Evans was convicted and sentenced to seven years' transportation.

For most of the time that he was London's finisher of the law, Thrift seems not to have had too bad a reputation generally. General Williamson, the Lieutenant of the Tower, even described him as 'a good sort of man' on one occasion: that was in a conversation with Lord Kilmarnock on the eve of the latter's execution. In March 1750, however, Thrift was himself in trouble again - and this time the trouble was more serious than any he had been in before.

On the 11th of that month, in the early evening, a man named David Faris, his wife Rebecca and two companions, Timothy Garvey and Patrick Farrel, were involved in a quarrel with Thrift and his wife outside the hangman's house in Coal Yard. It had apparently started as a result of a remark made by Farrel about 'Jack Ketch' within Mrs Thrift's hearing.

Thrift allegedly punched Farrel in the face two or three times, then got a hanger from inside the house and chased Farrel and Faris to Short's Gardens, the other side of Drury Lane. There he caught up with them and fighting broke out, with other people (friends or acquaintances of the hangman) joining in.

Rebecca Faris, who had a child in her arms, reached the scene while the affray was in progress, as did Timothy Garvey, but neither of them appear to have taken any part in it. Shortly after their arrival, Rebecca's husband was struck several times with the hanger and fatally injured. By this time, the disturbance had attracted a large crowd of onlookers.

When the fighting stopped, the injured man was taken to the home of Henry Fielding, the Bow Street magistrate (and author of *Tom Jones*), before whom he swore that his wounds had been inflicted by Thrift. He was then taken to hospital, where he died eight days later.

Thrift denied striking the fatal blows and an acquaintance of his named Enoch Stock claimed to have struck them himself. Both men were committed to Newgate, but Stock was at some stage released without trial. On 27 April, Thrift appeared for trial at the Old Bailey, charged with David Faris's murder. He pleaded not guilty.

The first three witnesses were Rebecca Faris, Timothy Garvey and Patrick Farrel. They all said that it was the prisoner who had struck the deceased with the hanger and made the attack out to have been entirely unprovoked. Farrel said Thrift had struck at him as well as Faris and that they had both used sticks to ward off the blows. He denied that either of them had struck any blows themselves.

The next three witnesses, Thomas Clutton, Alice Waring and Philip Lisle, had all seen Faris struck with the hanger and said it was Thrift who had struck him. Clutton, however, had also been present at the quarrel in Coal Yard and said that Farrel had then called the hangman's wife a whore several times. And he went on to contradict Farrel's claim that neither he nor Faris had struck any blows themselves.

'There were two men that ran fighting with the deceased and Farrel was one,' said this witness. 'I saw the sticks going as fast as they could go.'

Farrel was then questioned on this point and admitted that he and Faris had been fighting with Thrift and one other man. Rebecca Faris was also questioned on the same point, but said she had not seen any fighting.

After Lisle had given evidence, Robert Heathfield, a surgeon at Westminster Infirmary, was called and told the court of Faris's condition when he was brought into the hospital. 'There was a piece cut out of the left side of his head, through the first table, flesh and all,' he said. 'There were four other wounds on different parts of his head and a wound on his left wrist. I imagined they were from some cutting instrument.' Heathfield also said that on two occasions during the time he was in hospital Faris had asserted that Thrift was the person who had caused his injuries.

Seven more prosecution witnesses followed, all of whom claimed that they had seen the prisoner attack the deceased. But Thrift then made a statement in his defence, in which he claimed that he had been assaulted himself and denied striking Faris. This, according to the *Sessions Papers*, is what he said:

'I had been twice at St Giles's Church that day, and as I was coming home through Drury Lane, Farrel began the quarrel. There were four of them: the deceased's wife was one, with a child in her arms. I turned into the Coal Yard where I live.

' "Blood and ounds," said Farrel. "Do you know who this is coming along?"

' "No," said the deceased. "I do not know him."

'He said again, "That is Jack Ketch. He stole a gold watch and two silver spoons and has broke out of Newgate."

'Said I, "Go along, you blackguard dog!"

'They said there was ten guineas reward for taking of me. Farrel knocked me down at my own door. I strove to take the stick out of his hand. The others of them gave me another blow and knocked me down again.

'I desired my wife to fetch the hanger and I do declare it never was out of the scabbard till Enoch Stock took it out.'

Having given his own version of events, Thrift called a man named Elliot to give evidence in support of it. Elliot, who had apparently been involved in the fighting, was a lodger at the prisoner's house and had, in recent weeks, been acting as hangman in his landlord's place. He corroborated parts of Thrift's story, claiming to have seen the prisoner being struck with a stick by one of the dead man's companions and to have seen Enoch Stock take the hanger from him before Faris was attacked with it.

He also said: 'After the fight was over, and the deceased was cut, I took the hanger from Enoch Stock and brought it to the prisoner's house.'

After Elliot, Thrift called four more witnesses. The first two, a woman named Patience Jones and a man named John Collison, both said they had seen Enoch Stock with the hanger in his hand. The former said that she saw him 'cutting at somebody'; the latter claimed that he saw him strike the deceased.

The next witness, William Cook, said he saw men fighting with sticks, but saw no hanger at all. He also said that one of the men had sworn that he would 'cut Jack Ketch's brains out'.

The last of the prisoner's witnesses was Enoch Stock. Stock's evidence fell short of a confession that he had killed Faris, but was nonetheless in the hangman's favour.

'On 11 March, I was drinking a pint of beer at a public-house in Drury Lane with a friend,' said Stock. 'About a quarter of an hour after five in the evening, I parted with him and was standing to make water.

'I heard a great noise, and I went up to the mob to see what was the matter, as far as the gateway near Short's Gardens. I heard the prisoner say, "You thieves! Have you a mind to murder me?" They were beating him with sticks, four of them. He said, "For God's sake, help me, for these rogues will kill me!"

'When he saw me, I had known him nineteen or twenty years. I did not see him hit any of them, but stood against the wall in a white flannel waistcoat. They knocked me down several times and broke my head in several places, also my little finger in defending my head.

'I was quite stunned and lost my senses. I strove to get up two or three times and they knocked me down again. I went home hanging on the prisoner's shoulder.'

The *Sessions Papers* state that the witness produced his bloodstained shirt in court and was then asked whether he saw the hanger. 'Yes,' he replied. 'But I do not know what became of it. I do not know how I got away, they beat me so unmercifully.'

Despite the evidence given by his five witnesses, and the unreliability of some of the prosecution witnesses on certain points, the prisoner's story was not believed and he was convicted of murder. When the sessions ended, he was sentenced to death.

* * *

Thrift spent the next few weeks in one of Newgate's condemned cells, awaiting his fate. The cell was one of fifteen built in the late 1720s, to take the place of the old Condemned Hold. They were situated in an annex to the prison, where they occupied three storeys.

In view of the gravity of his offence, it must have seemed at first that he had little chance of escaping the gallows. But he was initially reprieved for two weeks, then reprieved again 'during the Pleasure of the Lords of the Regency'. Finally, in September of the same year, he was granted a free pardon.

With so many offenders being hanged for comparatively minor crimes, it was quite extraordinary for a convicted murderer to be treated with such leniency. And it is even more amazing to discover that, on his release from prison, he was allowed to resume his duties as hangman.

'A Free Pardon came for John Thrift the Hangman, last Saturday... and he is to resume his Profession the next Execution,' reported the newspaper *Old England* on 22 September. The report hinted that, having become obnoxious to the Jacobites for his celebrated executions on Tower Hill and Kennington Common, he had been pardoned as a warning to them. Perhaps that was so.

Three days later, the *General Advertiser* informed its readers: 'Yesterday a Woman was whipped at the Cart's Tail, thro' Piccadilly (by John Thrift lately pardoned) pursuant to her Sentence, at the last Sessions at the Old Bailey.'

Later the same week, Thrift inflicted another such whipping, and the following week, on 3 October, he hanged twelve malefactors at Tyburn. The twelve included James Maclean, a wellknown highwayman who had had three thousand visitors in Newgate the day after he was condemned.

Shortly afterwards, it was reported that Thrift had been replaced as hangman, but this proved not to be true. He continued to hold the post until his death a year and a half later, when a man named Thomas Turlis was appointed to succeed him. Turlis, erroneously called Tullis, was reported to have been his deputy for many years.

* * *

Thrift's death took place on 5 May 1752, and he was buried six days later at St Paul's Churchyard, Covent Garden. It is not known why he was buried there rather than in his own parish of St Giles's-in-the-Fields, but it may have been feared that his funeral would attract a hostile crowd if he were interred locally.

In the event, it attracted a hostile crowd anyway: 'a great Concourse of People, who seemed so displeased with his being buried there, that the Attendants of the Funeral, among whom was Tullis, the present Hangman, were afraid that the

Body would be torn out of the Coffin', reported the *London Daily Advertiser*. Because of this, the body had to be carried into the church and kept there until the danger subsided. It was finally buried without incident about eight o'clock in the evening.

The hostility of the 'great concourse' was apparently due, not to the fact that Thrift had been a hangman, but to the fact that he had not been a resident of the Parish of St Paul's.

'It is remarkable, that by the great Number of Burials in that Church-yard, the Ground has been so much raised of late Years, that it advances near to the Parlour Windows of the adjoining Houses, to which it will in a short time reach, if they continue burying so fast from other Parishes,' the *Advertiser* explained.

8. Last London Hangmen of the Tyburn Era

Thomas Turlis may well have served as John Thrift's deputy, but claims in two newspapers that he had done so for 'many years' were clearly inaccurate. Only a little over two years earlier, Thrift's lodger, Elliot, had carried out executions at Tyburn while the hangman himself was in jail, so Turlis was obviously not his deputy at that time. His length of service in that capacity could therefore only have been two years at the most.

Turlis was, however, appointed to succeed Thrift as hangman within a short time of the post becoming vacant. He then took on a Joseph Barnet to serve as *his* deputy, but Barnet proved not to be at all reliable. On 23 May 1752, *Read's Weekly Journal or British-Gazetteer* reported:

> Tuesday a Man was committed to Newgate by Sir George Champion for stealing a Cask of Snuff. He was Deputy to Thomas Tullis (*sic*), who a few Days since succeeded the late John Thrift as publick Executioner.

Barnet appeared for trial at the Old Bailey a month later. The *Sessions Papers* reveal that the crime had taken place on 16 April and that the prosecutor's name was Francis Devall; the stolen cask was valued at 4d and its contents at £7. Further details of the crime are given as follows:

> As Joseph Smith, a carman, was going with his cart from the custom house to the prosecutor's with the snuff and other goods, he rested his cart by the way to carry a parcel to another gentleman's house. When he returned he missed the cask of snuff. The prisoner, and another person who made his escape, were detected in selling it in Shoemaker Row.

In a case of this type, stealing to the value of 40s was then a capital offence. But, as in Marvell's case, the jury undervalued the goods in order to bring the prisoner in guilty without putting his life at risk. Convicted of stealing to the value of 39s, Barnet was sentenced to seven years' transportation.

Turlis's career, of course, was unaffected by Barnet's conviction and he remained hangman of London for the next nineteen years. During that time, he probably had a succession of deputies or assistants, none of whom we know anything about.

Turlis, according to *The Hangmen of England*, was himself in trouble with the law on one occasion, after being caught stealing coals from a neighbour's cellar. The hangman and his family had apparently been living in extreme poverty - we are not told where - due to a recent decline in the number of executions. Because of this, the sheriffs intervened on his behalf and prevented him from being punished. At the same time, they arranged for him to be given the additional post of hangman of Surrey, which was then vacant.

The source of this story is, unfortunately, unknown. The one Bleackley gives is *Lloyd's Evening Post* of 15 January 1763, but this is incorrect: *Lloyd's* was actually not published that day and a search of other issues (and other newspapers) published about the same time has failed to unearth the report in question.

So, although it is true that Turlis was hangman of Surrey, as well as London and Middlesex, during the latter part of his career, it has to be admitted that we do not know whether there is any truth in Bleackley's story of how he came to be appointed to the post.

*   *   *

During the first seven years that Turlis was the London hangman, executions at Tyburn were still carried out on the Triple Tree. In 1759, however, this was pulled down, and for the next twenty-four years a 'new moving gallows' was used in place of it.

The new gallows, which had only one crossbeam, was first used on 3 October 1759, for the hanging of four offenders. The most notable execution carried out on it was that of Earl Ferrers, a peer of the realm who was hanged on 5 May the following year for the murder of his steward.

Ferrers had been imprisoned in the Tower of London and tried before the House of Lords. The procession to Tyburn for his execution was the grandest ever, with the condemned riding in his own landau, drawn by six horses.

Hangings at Tyburn were generally still carried out from the backs of carts, but for this particular one a scaffold with a raised platform had been constructed. The scaffold was covered with black baize and, as always when the condemned was a nobleman, the executioner had to ask his forgiveness for what he was about to do.

Ferrers had five guineas for Turlis, but gave it to his assistant by mistake. This caused an undignified dispute between the two men, which one of the sheriffs had to settle, presumably by making the assistant give the money to the person for

Under an Act of Parliament passed in 1751, all persons convicted of murder were to be executed on the second day after conviction and their bodies afterwards hung in chains or anatomized. The first to suffer under it was Thomas Wilford, a one-armed youth of seventeen who was hanged at Tyburn on 2 July 1752 for killing his wife in a fit of jealousy. His body was dissected.

Dr Archibald Cameron on his way to Tyburn in 1753, to be executed for treason (from *The Annals of Newgate*).

The hanging of Earl Ferrers for the murder of his steward (from an old print).

whom it was intended.

The platform on which the condemned man had to stand was about a yard square and eighteen inches above the floor of the scaffold. The signal for it to be lowered was given by the sheriff who had settled the dispute, as the prisoner refused to give it himself.

Due to a fault in the mechanism, the platform did not fall as far as it should have done, and the condemned man's toes went on touching it. Turlis and his assistant had therefore to pull his legs, to bring his suffering to an end.

When the body was cut down, the hangman and his assistant fought for possession of the rope. This was not made of silk, as some accounts state, but was still valuable, as it could be sold by the inch in some nearby tavern.

The use of the raised platform was never repeated at Tyburn, where, after Ferrers's execution, the authorities went back to hanging offenders from the backs of carts. This method continued to be used there until 1783, when 'Tyburn Fair' was held for the last time. By then, Thomas Turlis had been dead for twelve years.

*   *   *

Three years after the execution of Earl Ferrers, again at Tyburn, Turlis was involved in a struggle with an Irishwoman named Hannah Dagoe, who had been sentenced to death for theft.

Hannah was one of three offenders who were to be hanged that day, the others being Paul Lewis, a young highwayman, and John Rice, a stockbroker who had been convicted of forgery. At the place of execution, she managed to free herself from the rope binding her arms and put up a fierce fight, almost knocking the hangman out of the cart. She also tore off her hat, cloak and gloves and threw them out among the spectators, to prevent Turlis himself from having them after her death.

With much difficulty (for nobody tried to help him), the hangman eventually got Hannah's wrists tied together and the rope round her neck - upon which, she threw herself out of the cart. As a result, her neck was broken and she died instantly.

Hannah Dagoe's execution took place on 4 May 1763, before a great crowd of people. James Boswell was among the spectators, watching from a nearby scaffold. 'I was most terribly shocked, and thrown into a very deep melancholy,' he recorded in his diary.

On 5 December the same year, Turlis had another misadventure, this time at the public burning of a seditious publication, the *North Briton* no. 45, at the Royal Exchange. The burning caused a riot, during which the mob threw dirt at the hangman and other officials who were present, then rushed at them and drove them from the scene.

Five years later, Turlis was stoned by spectators at a triple hanging in King-ston. The *Public Advertiser* of 20 April 1768, reporting the incident, stated that the hangman had been 'much hurt and bruised' during the attack.

And on 6 March the following year, the same newspaper reported another such occurrence, this time at the pillorying of a perjurer in Southwark:

> On Friday, a tradesman, convicted of wilful and corrupt perjury, stood in and upon the Pillory in High Street, Southwark, and was severely treated by the populace. They also pelted Turlis, the executioner, with stones and brickbats, which cut him in the Head and Face in a terrible manner.

But despite the dangers to which his work exposed him, Turlis continued as hangman until his death in 1771. The last time he officiated at Tyburn was on 27 March of that year, when five offenders were hanged. The *Gentleman's Magazine* tells us that on that occasion 'Birch, Sidey, Mortis, and Peak behaved in the press yard in a most audacious manner, and struck the Executioner when put into the cart'. Early in April, Turlis died while on his way back to London after attending the Surrey Assizes at Kingston.

Turlis, often called Tullis or Tollis in the newspapers, was, like John Hooper, a literate man: a sample of *his* handwriting is also reproduced in *The Hangmen of England*. The handwriting in this case is from a bill presented by Turlis to the Sheriff of Middlesex at midsummer 1767.

This document shows that the County of Middlesex paid half of the salary (£5 a quarter) which Turlis received as hangman of London *and* Middlesex, so the other half was obviously claimed separately from the Sheriff of London. As he was also hangman of Surrey, the sheriff of that county would have had to pay him a salary as well.

The bill also shows that the fees which Turlis received for inflicting whippings varied from 5s to 10s. As it makes no mention of any executions, it is clear that he had already been paid for all the Middlesex prisoners he had hanged during the quarter in question.

In addition to his salary and fees, the bill includes a claim for 7s 6d for hiring a horse, which Turlis probably needed for whippings carried out at the cart's tail. It does not, however, include any claim for payment towards the cost of employing an assistant, which he was obliged to meet out of his own pocket.

* * *

The next known hangman of London was Edward Dennis, the last person to hold the post during the Tyburn era. Dennis was also the last London hangman to be convicted of a capital offence.

APRIL SESSIONS, 1767.

	£	s	d
Horsewhipping May the 4th.		7	6
For whipping of George Cane at Isleworth.		10	0
For whipping of Elizabeth Fletcher.		5	0
For whipping of George Cane at Isleworth.		10	0

JUNE SESSIONS.

	£	s	d
For whipping of Sarah Johnson.		5	0
For whipping of Anne Eaton.		5	0
For whipping of Timothy McCarthy from one end of the Haymarket to the other end.		5	0
For whipping of Mary Dolley, from Cavendish Square to Duke Street, Tyburn Road.		10	0
Horse hiring, June the 10th.		7	6
For whipping of Abraham Johnson from Mile End Turnpike to London Hospital.		10	0
For whipping of Jane Hodgson from one end of Nightingale Lane to the other end.		5	0
For a Quarter's wages due at Midsummer.	2	10	0
	6	10	0

Turlis's bill in respect of money owed to him by the Sheriff of Middlesex at midsummer 1767.

It is not clear whether he was appointed to succeed Turlis or whether he acceded to the post at a later date. Bleackley claims that he *did* succeed him, but there seems to be no evidence of this. He must, however, have been appointed before 1775, for by then a William Brunskill had begun serving as his deputy. Brunskill was to remain deputy hangman of London until Dennis's death, when he was appointed finisher of the law himself.

In June 1780, Dennis was involved in the Gordon Riots. These lasted for several days, with mobs rampaging through the city, causing widespread destruction. The homes of many Catholics and Catholic sympathizers were ransacked and burnt; other buildings which were destroyed included Newgate Prison, which had recently been rebuilt. The prison was attacked and set on fire on 6 June, the rioters releasing hundreds of its inmates, including a number of capital offenders who had been due to be hanged two days later.

In *Barnaby Rudge*, Dickens gives Dennis an important role in the attack on

It is reported, that while one of the malefactors who was executed yesterday, was exhorting the populace to take warning by his untimely end, he in a very particular manner pointed his address towards a certain gentleman who presided at the fatal ceremony, whose conscious blush upon the occasion it was observed betrayed some glimmerings of grace, and gave hopes that he might possibly avail himself of so solemn an admonition.

The Middlesex Journal, 15-17 October 1771.

Newgate, but in real life, as far as we know, he had nothing to do with it. He did, however, take part in a riot in Holborn the following day and was apprehended in connection with this and other riots a few days later. The *London Chronicle* of 15-17 June reported that he had been committed to New Prison, Clerkenwell, on the 14th, having been 'charged on oath with being principally concerned in several of the late lawless depredations committed by the populace, particularly at a chandler's shop in New Turnstile'. The shop referred to was part of the chandler's house, the whole of which had been destroyed on the evening of 7 June; the chandler's name was Edmund Boggis.

On 3 July, the hangman appeared for trial at the Old Bailey, charged with feloniously assembling 'with twenty other persons, and more' and assisting in the demolition of Mr Boggis's house. He pleaded not guilty.

The prosecution called four witnesses who had seen the prisoner on the evening in question. It was clear from their evidence that he had taken an active part in the destruction, carrying articles of furniture and pieces of the woodwork from Mr Boggis's house and burning them on a nearby fire. One of these witnesses, in answer to a question from the prisoner himself, said that Dennis had been 'the most active person amongst the whole mob'.

Edmund Boggis was also called. He told the court that the mob had arrived at his home between six and seven o'clock in the evening and that he had then left the house because he was afraid to stay there. The house had been in good repair when he left, but when he returned he found it had been 'torn almost all to pieces', he said. During the course of his evidence, Mr Boggis also said that he had seen the prisoner taking part in the destruction of a public-house in the same neighbourhood the previous night.

Dennis denied having been one of the rioters, but admitted carrying wood from Mr Boggis's house to the fire, claiming that he had done so under duress. He said that he had been out to see a friend that day and had run into the mob on the way back to his home in Newtoners Street, just a short distance from New Turnstile. Some of the rioters had then seized him and forced him to help them.

OLD BAILEY.

The Court was taken up from ten o'clock in the morning, till five in the afternoon, with the trials of only two prisoners.

The one was *Edward Dennis*, alias *Jack Ketch*; he was tried for having assisted in demolishing the house of Mr. *Boggis* in New Turnstile, Holborn. The witnesses did not prove that they saw the prisoner enter the house, or come out of it; but they positively declared, that they saw him come from that quarter where the house stood, and carry some furniture on his shoulders, which he threw into the fire.

The prisoner admitted the facts attested by the witnesses, but pleaded compulsion as his defence. He said, that passing near where the fire was, on his way home, he was known by some of the mob, who told their comrades that he was *bloody* Jack Ketch, and that he was sorry that by the breaking open of Newgate, he had lost a job, meaning the execution of the prisoners who were to have been hanged on Thursday the 8th of June. He replied to the mob, that he was glad the convicts had escaped; and wished they might not come in his way again. The mob, however, not satisfied, insisted that he should be as criminal as they were; and swore, that if he would not join them in burning the goods, they would throw him into the fire. Apprehending every thing from their fury, he consented to all they required, wishing to trust his life to the judgment and mercy of that Court, sooner than to the ungovernable fury of a mob.

The Recorder who tried the prisoner, gave to this defence as much weight, as any defence could admit of, that rested solely on the declaration of a prisoner. Nay he went farther, and admitted the circumstances urged by the prisoner, as probable, on account of the odious light in which Dennis stood, as executioner for London and Middlesex.

The jury, however, could not overturn the positive evidence of three or four witnesses, for an unsupported defence; and consequently brought in their verdict, GUILTY, DEATH. The prisoner threw himself on his knees, implored fervently for mercy, declared his will was innocent, because his body had been compelled; that he had been even thrown on his face by the mob; and appealed to the Sheriffs, Aldermen, and Lord Mayor, to vouch that his general character had been that of a peaceable quiet man.

The *Morning Post's* report of Dennis's conviction.

> It is somewhat remarkable, that the two worthies, Jack Ketch and Lying Dick
> should in the same day be under the same misfortune, in calling witnesses to their
> character who would not appear.
>
> *The London Courant and Westminster Chronicle*, 5 July 1780.

'They made me carry wood several times, and I huzzaed by their orders several times,' said Dennis. 'They swore they would use me ill if I did not.' And he added: 'I kept myself from all other riots: I never was found out at a late hour. I was always abed before candlelight during the riots, because I would keep from the mob. I was vastly afraid of them: I knew they would use me ill.'

The prisoner also claimed: 'I have served the sheriffs a good while and they never heard any bad character of me.'

Though Dennis's defence rested solely upon his own declaration, the judge advised the jury that his version of events was a probable one, in view of the 'odious light' in which he stood as executioner for London and Middlesex. The jurors, however, were not swayed by this and, after considering the evidence for about ten minutes, they brought in a verdict of guilty.

Dennis, like many of his fellow rioters, was sentenced to death. But he was not hanged (except in *Barnaby Rudge*): in fact, just two days after he was condemned his sentence was respited 'during his Majesty's pleasure'. And within a matter of weeks he was granted a free pardon and returned to his duties as hangman.

'The humanity of Mr. Smith, the keeper of Tothillfields bridewell, to whose custody he was committed, deserves due praise,' says the *Gentleman's Magazine* account of Dennis's conviction. 'He declined confining him among the other prisoners lest his obnoxious character should expose him to their rage.'

* * *

In all, sixty-two of the rioters were condemned, and of these twenty-five were actually hanged. These executions all took place during the four or five weeks following the suppression of the disturbances, and the prisoners concerned were all hanged at or near the scenes of their crimes. Four other offenders who were hanged during the course of those weeks suffered at Tyburn in the usual way.

Brunskill, as deputy hangman, officiated at some of these executions - he is referred to in one report as 'Deputy Jack Ketch' - but Dennis was apparently released in time to hang some of the rioters himself. About this time, however, there were a number of incidents at the gallows which must have given the sheriffs cause for concern.

On 22 July, the *Public Advertiser* reported that a 'very singular and most shocking Circumstance' had occurred at a triple hanging in Old Street the previous day. After the condemned had hung for the usual time and their bodies were being cut down, the cap of one of them was removed, either by accident or by design, in full view of the crowds. The incident caused much hissing among the spectators, some of whom were sure that the face of the corpse had been exposed to them deliberately.

Three days later, reporting another triple execution, the same newspaper had a more serious complaint:

A Correspondent, who was a Spectator of the Execution of the three unfortunate Criminals at Tyburn on Saturday last, says he was exceedingly shocked to perceive the Torture and Agony in which two of them died, owing to the Knot of the Rope slipping. Some of the unhappy Rioters were also equally agonized by the same Circumstance. The Executioner therefore should be more careful; for although he appears, himself, to have as little Feeling as the Rope or Gallows by which he earns his Bread, yet there are others who can sympathize with their miserable Fellow Creatures, when at the moment of launching into Eternity, and who feel the keenest Anguish of Soul at seeing them thus tortured.

And on 11 August the *Public Advertiser* described 'the present Jack Ketch' as a disgrace to his office, saying that he handled the condemned 'with as little Concern as a Butcher would a Sheep or Bullock'. 'On Wednesday last he threw off the Hat of one of the unfortunate Sufferers, in a Manner that merited the severest Censure; and for other brutal Acts, he was much (booed) by the Populace,' the newspaper asserted.

These bunglings and offences against decency were all quite grave and it is likely that 'the present Jack Ketch' was reprimanded over them - and perhaps even threatened with dismissal - on more than one occasion. He was, however, kept on in his post and he and Brunskill went on working together, without - as far as we know - any further interruption, for the next six years.

One other item of interest from the *Public Advertiser* of that year is a paragraph about the hangman's income, which adds a little to what we already know from Turlis's bill to the Sheriff of Middlesex thirteen years earlier. The paragraph, which was published on 14 July, states that his salary was £30 a year (for Dennis, like Turlis, was hangman of Surrey, as well as London and Middlesex) and that he was paid 6s 8d for each person executed and 5s for every public whipping. It also mentions his 'other advantages', but without giving any details of them.

The number of people hanged at any one time in London during Dennis's tenure of office was between one and twenty; the hangman's fees for his services on any one hanging day must therefore have totalled between 6s 8d and £6 13s 4d.

There was actually only one occasion when twenty were hanged: that was in 1785. But multiple executions were far more frequent than single ones and there were quite a number of times when the number hanged was ten or more.

Although Dennis had no noblemen to execute, his perquisites still included occasional gratuities from the condemned. One prisoner who had money for him was Francis Henry de la Motte, a traitor who was hanged, drawn and quartered at Tyburn in 1781. Unfortunately, like Earl Ferrers, De la Motte inadvertently caused an unpleasant scene by giving it to the wrong person.

The incident in this case occurred at Newgate - then still in the process of being restored - while the condemned man was being prepared for the procession to the gallows. For some reason, he thought that an official tying his arms was the hangman and gave him five guineas that he had intended for Dennis. Dennis, who was present, demanded the money, and a heated argument started. At De la Motte's request, the other man was finally forced to give it to him.

Towards the end of 1783, while Dennis was still hangman, Tyburn was used as a place of execution for the last time. Thereafter, with some exceptions, the condemned of London and Middlesex were hanged at Newgate itself, on a site at the front of the prison. Execution Dock, however, continued to be used for the hanging of maritime offenders until well into the nineteenth century.

The New Drop, as the Newgate gallows was initially called, was first used on 9 December 1783, when ten people were hanged together. A portable structure with a scaffold and a falling platform, it was erected, when needed, outside the Debtors' Door, at right angles to the prison wall. Over the next few years, it was replaced or modified several times, but the site itself continued to be used for hangings until 1868.

Executions at Newgate, like those at Tyburn, were often attended by very large crowds. Quite often they filled not only the space at the front of the jail, but the streets adjacent to it as well.

*   *   *

Edward Dennis continued as hangman for three years after the new site came into use. In 1785, according to a contemporary source (*The Attic Miscellany*, 1791), the sheriffs gave him a robe of some sort, but he didn't like wearing it and eventually sold it. The person who bought it from him was a fortune-teller known as 'Old Cain'.

On 22 November the following year, Dennis was reported to have died 'at his apartments in the Old Bailey' the previous day. Announcing his death, the *Daily Universal Register* (afterwards *The Times*) referred facetiously to 'his office of Finisher of the Law, Surveyor of the New-drop, and Apparitor of the Necklace, alias Yeoman of the Halter, &c.', and claimed that he had, on his deathbed,

The hanging of ten people at Newgate Prison (from *The Old Bailey Chronicle*, 1783-4, by James Mountague).

'recommended his son to the succession'. The hangman was buried four days later, in the churchyard of St Giles's-in-the-Fields.

It is not known whether Dennis really wanted his son to succeed him, but if he did, his wishes were ignored. The next hangman of London was William Brunskill, who carried out a multiple hanging at Newgate on the day after his predecessor's death. He was to hold the post for the next twenty-eight years.

9. A Dumfries Hangman and His Dues

Roger Wilson was the last but one hangman of Dumfries. He, too, was a long-serving functionary.

Wilson's appointment to the post took place on 17 April 1758, but was backdated to 3 August the previous year. The Town Council Minutes show that he agreed to serve the town as its 'Executioner or Common Dempster' for the rest of his life, unless the Council at any time saw cause to dismiss him.*

He did, in fact, retain the post until shortly before his death twenty-seven years later. For part of that time he was also the local town crier, to which additional post he was appointed on 23 December 1760.

Wilson, an illiterate man, was evidently a native of the village of Glencairn, in the same county. He was born about 1710, and so must have been about forty-eight when he became hangman.

Executions were rare occurrences in Dumfries, but Wilson, like other hangmen of his time, had lesser punishments to inflict as well. These included the pillorying of a thief named William Hannah in 1770, on which occasion a disturbance broke out and Wilson and another burgh officer were injured by missiles thrown by spectators. The Council Minutes tell us that he was then aged sixty and also that he was married. This, however, is all that is known for certain about his personal circumstances.

As hangman, Wilson received a salary of £6 a year, in addition to having a free house at the town's expense. As town crier, he was paid a further salary of £1 a year.

As hangman, he also had the right to take a ladleful of the contents of every sack of meal, peas, beans, potatoes or any other such commodity in the town's markets: a perquisite which Wilson himself claimed was worth upwards of £13 a year in the early 1780s.

This custom was by no means peculiar to Dumfries. At one time, as mentioned in the first chapter, the hangman of Edinburgh had had the right to take a *lock*, or handful, of meal out of every sack of this produce in the city market. This had since been abolished and replaced by an increase in salary, as had a similar right which had formerly existed in Glasgow.

But in other Scottish towns the finisher of the law still enjoyed rights of this type. An advertisement for a Haddington hangman, published in the *Edinburgh Evening Courant* of 4 July 1772, states: 'He will have £3 Sterling of wages

---

* Wilson's forename is spelt 'Rodger' in the Council Minutes, but 'Roger' in Court of Session records (see p. 187).

10 Octr
1781

Unto the Honble the Sheriff Deputy of the Shire of
Dumfries and the Magistrates of the Burgh of
Dumfries

     The Petition of Roger Wilson Common Executioner for
the Burgh of Dumfries;

Humbly Sheweth   That the petitioner has a right in virtue
of his office to levy for his own use out of each load
of meal exposed to sale in the mealmarket of Dumfries one laddlefull of meal of the size or measure
immemorially used by the Petitioner and his
predecessors in office containing about a chopin and
a Gill Liquid measure

     That notwithstanding the Petitioners said
right sundry persons

have brought to the said market for sale this
tenth   day of October 1781 sundry loads
of Oat meal but refuse to Allow the Petitioner
to levy his usual dues —

     May it therefore please your Honours
to grant warrant for bring the said
Persons   — before you and to
grant warrant to your Officers for
pounding as much of the said meal as
will satisfy the Petitioners usual due
with what more you shall be pleased
to modify as the expences of this
application or otherways to grant
warrant for imprisoning the said
Persons till payment of such a
sum as you shall modify to be the worth
and value of the said Customary duty &
expences according to Justice &ca —

           Roger   Wilson

yearly, a free house, new cloaths; and his perquisites in meal, wool and calling of fish, greens, and other commodities, are very considerable.' We also find, in the *Aberdeen Journal* of 8 June 1789:

> Wanted immediately, at Elgin, A COMMON EXECUTIONER. He will have a free house, and about two acres of land, a number of perquisites payable out of the commodities sold in town, and a considerable salary.

And in Inverness, as will be seen in Chapter 17, he also had a variety of such perquisites: possibly even more than in Haddington or Elgin.

Roger Wilson's dues were nonetheless resented by local farmers and meal-sellers and from time to time one of the dealers would refuse to open his sacks to him. When that happened, the person concerned would be examined by the Dean of Dumfries, or by one of the town's other magistrates, and would be warned that he was in danger of being sent to jail. That was usually enough to induce him to pay the hangman his dues.

One day, however - it was 1 August 1781 - a rebellious dealer named John Johnston refused to allow Wilson to take any of his meal even *after* being warned, so the Dean, Nicol Shaw, committed him to prison. There he was held for the next two hours or so, until the magistrates decided that he had been punished enough and ordered that he be set free.

Some weeks later, on 10 October of that year, Wilson arrived at the meal market with his brass ladle, only to find that *none* of the dealers would allow him to levy his dues. Wilson then obtained a warrant from the magistrates and the Sheriff Deputy of the county, giving him formal authority to demand payment, and a party of burgh and sheriff's officers went back to the market with him, to help him to execute it. But the dealers were united against him and his return led to disorderly scenes. Before long, the dealers tied up their sacks and left, so that Wilson still received no meal dues at all that day.

Shortly after this, John Johnston began legal proceedings against the magistrates of Dumfries, challenging the legality of the executioner's dues. He also sought damages for wrongous imprisonment against those involved in his brief incarceration on 1 August. But the action was defended and proved to be ill advised.

Although Johnston was the pursuer in these proceedings, it soon became clear that others had instigated them and were helping him financially. Johnston himself was a man of slender means and could not have afforded the costs of such an action on his own.

Opposite: Roger Wilson's petition of 10 October 1781, craving powers to enforce payment of his dues (reproduced by kind permission of the Keeper of the Records of Scotland).

The dispute appeared three times before the Court of Session in Edinburgh. At its second appearance, in June 1782, the court rejected Johnston's case; the magistrates then claimed expenses and these were awarded against Johnston on 8 February the following year.

The case papers relating to this dispute still exist and run to over 600 pages. There is no record of what happened to Johnston afterwards, but he was almost certainly ruined by the action and probably ended up in prison for debt.

Roger Wilson went on serving as hangman for another two and a half years, but on 1 August 1785, at the age of about seventy-five, he was reported to be dying. A search was then started for someone to replace him and on 23 August one Joseph Tait was appointed to the post. Wilson finally died on 21 September, and the following day the Town Council agreed to pay his funeral costs.

Robert Chambers's article on Scottish executioners (see pp. 32-3), published in 1834, says that Wilson's wife at some stage hanged herself; it also claims that the hangman's two daughters, having left Dumfries to escape the stigma attached to their name, both eventually married above their station in life. But none of this appears to be confirmed by any contemporary record, so it may all be untrue.

Joseph Tait was appointed to serve as hangman only during the Council's pleasure, but was kept on for over twenty years. On 16 December 1786, he was imprisoned for debt, but the Council secured his release a month later. On 14 December 1789, his salary was increased to £10 a year, after many complaints that it was too low to provide for the needs of his family and himself.

One of the reasons for his poverty was that the hangman's market dues no longer had the same value as they had had a few years earlier. Following the rejection of Johnston's claims by the Court of Session, these exactions continued to cause resentment among the town's meal-dealers, some of whom now avoided payment by selling their commodities in shops or houses instead of taking them to the marketplace.

The Council Minutes show that in addition to increasing his salary, the Council recommended that Joseph Tait should begin legal proceedings against the dealers concerned, with the town paying his expenses. But when he tried to do this, the hangman could find no solicitor willing to take on the case. The Council then lost patience with him and withdrew its support, a decision recorded in the minutes for 20 December as follows:

> The Said Day there was a petition given to the Councill by Joseph Tait the Touns Executioner showing that he had got an action of the Meal Sellers but he is not able to prosecute them as he says none of the writers* in Toun will take the plea in hand and desiring the Touns assistance in the matter which petition being heard in

---

* Writers to the Signet (solicitors).

Councill and considered they refuse the desire thereof and certify the petitioner that the Councill will not be troubled with any more petitions of the like nature altho they have permitted this day to prosecute all the Meal Sellers in Dumfries if he inclines and at his own expenses.

Tait nonetheless continued to levy his dues in the marketplace for the next six years. Then, early in 1796, the town was plunged into a food shortage, as a result of several years of poor harvests. The shortage led to a number of disturbances.

The Dumfries authorities issued an address to the farmers of the district, requesting them to bring all their spare stocks into the town, to be sold in the market without delay. The farmers were willing to do this, but as soon as the sacks of produce were set out for sale, Tait appeared with his ladle and began dipping it into each of them in turn.

To avoid losing the co-operation of the farmers, the Town Council then hastily abolished the hangman's dues, giving him a further increase in salary of £2 a year as compensation for his losses.

* * *

Joseph Tait continued as hangman of Dumfries until 1808, when the post itself was abolished. By that time, his salary had risen to £18 a year, payable, as always, in quarterly instalments.

10. A Miscellany

In the mid-1660s, the town of Irvine, on the Ayrshire coast, had a hangman named William Sutherland, whose story is told in Robert Wodrow's *History of the Sufferings of the Church of Scotland* (1721-2).

Sutherland was a poor man from Strathnaven in northern Scotland. He had arrived in Irvine about 1661, after four years of cattle-herding in other parts of the country, and had begun acting as hangman while out of work.

During his first year or two in the town, however, he had learnt to read and had begun to study the Bible. This had a profound effect upon him and caused him to have serious misgivings about his work. 'I began to scruple to execute any, except I was clear they deserved to die,' he says in an autobiographical sketch published as an appendix to Wodrow's history.

In December 1666, Sutherland was ordered by the Provost of Irvine to go to Ayr (the hangman of that town having fled), to hang eight Covenanters who had taken up arms in defence of their religion. He refused to do so.

Taken to Ayr by force, he was held in captivity, threatened with torture and even subjected to a mock execution by shooting. But Sutherland, who regarded the rebels as 'godly men', still refused to hang them, and eventually one of the condemned, named Cornelius Anderson, was prevailed upon to execute the others in return for a pardon for himself.

Anderson performed this grim duty, under the influence of drink, on 27 December 1666, and hanged another two Covenanters in Irvine on the 31st. A few days after that, Anderson himself died (according to Wodrow) 'in Distraction and great Misery'.

William Sutherland was kept in prison in Ayr for several weeks longer and was then released. Unfortunately, Wodrow does not tell us what became of him afterwards.

* * *

John Dalgleish was hangman of Edinburgh for twenty-six years. His appointment to the post, on 25 July 1722, followed the dismissal of his predecessor, Donald Sutherland (the Town Council Minutes say that he was 'suspended') for 'several misdemeanours'. Sutherland had been hangman only since 9 August the previous year.

Dalgleish had previously worked as a waterman. At his death in 1748, he was reported to have been between seventy and eighty years old: he must therefore have been middle-aged when he embarked on his new career.

Edinburgh, of course, had many executions during the time that Dalgleish was hangman, but nowhere near the number carried out at Tyburn during the same period: the total was in dozens rather than hundreds. Sometimes many months elapsed between one hanging and the next.

The number of whippings in Edinburgh was also considerably lower than the number in London. So Dalgleish's annual income was obviously only a fraction of that enjoyed by Richard Arnet or John Hooper.

In addition to his salary and fees, however, the Edinburgh hangman, like most other Scottish executioners of the time, did have a free house. This was a small house in the Fishmarket Close (the Old Fishmarket Close, as it was later called): a building which was to be occupied by successive Edinburgh hangmen until almost the middle of the next century. It is not known how long it had been used for this purpose before Dalgleish's time.

The most notable hangings at which Dalgleish officiated were those of Margaret Dickson, a young woman convicted of murdering her new-born child, and Andrew Wilson, a smuggler condemned for robbing an excise office.

Margaret Dickson was a native of Musselburgh, a small town six miles to the east of Edinburgh. She was hanged in the Grassmarket on 2 September 1724, but was found to be still alive after being cut down and given to a group of her friends for burial. No fresh attempt was made to hang her and she made a full recovery.

Andrew Wilson's execution took place twelve years later, on 14 April 1736. On that occasion, a disturbance broke out and the City Guard, commanded by

---

Wigtoune, Apryle 15th, 1685.

Councell Extraordinar.

the 91k Day, the bailzie and Councelors present, having convened John Malroy, hangman, befoir thcm, and examined him what was his reason to absent himself at this tym when ther was employment for him, he acknowledged he was in the wrong and was seduced yto; but now acknowledged himself the tounes ssrt (servant) and promised to byd (abide) be his service; but aledged that he had noe benefit or cellarie (salary) for his service and craved to have som allowance for tyme coming; Which he refered to the toun councell at ane frequent (early) meiting efter the provest's returne from Edr.; and in the meintym the bailzie, with advice and consent of the Councell, appoints the thessrer (treasurer) to furnish four shilling Scots (equal to fourpence sterling) ilk day to the sd. John Malroy dureing his abod in prissone.

From the minutes of the Town Council of Wigtown, the county town of Wigtownshire, south-west Scotland (*Notes and Queries*, 14th Series, CLVII, 299).

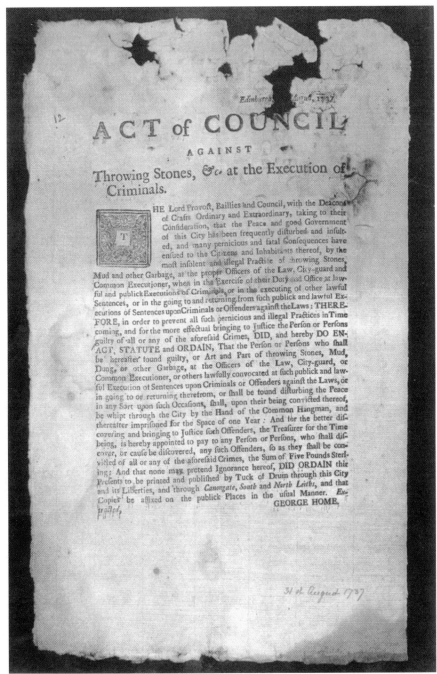

By courtesy of Edinburgh City Archives

An official notice published in Edinburgh in 1737, warning the populace against throwing stones and other objects at executions.

At Kirkcudbright, on the 3d current, died Janet Newall, aged 84 years. She was the last of the family of John Newall, who held the respectable situation of hangman in the town of Kirkcudbright for many years, and who never had an opportunity of exercising the important duties of his office excepting on one solitary occasion, in the year 1750. Besides Janet, the hangman had two other children, Elizabeth and William. Elizabeth, commonly called 'Lizzie Newall,' was a well-known character in Kirkcudbright.

The Times, 25 December 1835.

Captain John Porteous, fired on the crowd. Six people were killed outright and others died later of their injuries.

Porteous was tried for murder, convicted and sentenced to death. But as he awaited his fate, an angry mob overran the city, dragged him from the Tolbooth and lynched him in the Grassmarket. Only two people were ever tried for taking part in this outrage and both were acquitted.

Minor punishments inflicted by Dalgleish sometimes included mutilation, as we see from a report published in *The Weekly Journal or British Gazetteer* of 18 May 1728:

Edinburgh, May 9. Yesterday, by Order of the Magistrates, a Woman was whipt down the City, nail'd to the Tron, then had a Bit pinch'd out of her Nose with a new invented Machine, and was after sent to the House of Correction, for Thieving, House-breaking, and other wicked Practices.

Other minor tasks performed by Dalgleish included the public burning of inanimate objects. One such case was reported in the *London Journal* of 9 August 1729, as follows:

Edinburgh, July 31. Yesterday, by Warrant of the Magistrates, a Hair-Merchant who had carried on a Practice of cheating the Wigmakers with Wool mixt with Horse Hair, and selling it for human Hair, was imprisoned, and his Cargo burnt at the Cross by the Common Hangman.

In another case, reported in the *Caledonian Mercury* of 29 March 1742, 'a Sedan or Chair, with all its Accoutrements, was burnt at the Cross by the Common Executioner, having been stopt at the Netherbow-port with a dead Corpse in it some Weeks ago'. Two men who had been apprehended in connection with the affair were banished from the city.

And on 4 June 1746 Dalgleish performed yet another noteworthy duty when he took part in an official procession through the city, carrying the defeated Young

Pretender's standard.

Dalgleish died at his house in the Fishmarket Close on 14 July 1748, and was buried in the Greyfriars Churchyard on the night of the 15th. A report of his death in the *Caledonian Mercury* refers to him as 'honest John Dalgleish' and says that he was 'a Man all along famed for being conscientious to a Degree in the Exercise of his Office'.

Dalgleish's successor was apparently David Drummond, who was not appointed until 28 December the same year. Drummond lasted only until 8 March 1749, when he was replaced by a man named James Alexander.

*   *   *

Andrew Boyle, a former soldier, became hangman of Edinburgh on 1 July 1767, but was removed from the post in ignominious circumstances in February the following year. During the seven months or so that he was employed by the Town Council, he did not have a single execution to carry out.

The circumstances in which Boyle left the post are described in an advertisement which the city magistrates published in Edinburgh newspapers on 27 February 1768. The notice reads as follows:

> WHEREAS on the evening of Wednesday the 24th of February inst. ANDREW BOYLE, late common Executioner in this city, who was lately committed to the city guard, on suspicion of having committed sundry thefts in and about the city, found means to escape out of the guard-house, disguised in his wife's cloaths, who had been admitted to see him there. The Magistrates hereby promise a REWARD of FIVE GUINEAS, to any person or persons, who shall apprehend and secure the said Andrew Boyle in any prison in Scotland, within three months of this date.
>
> Boyle is a man about five feet eight inches high, smooth faced, of a dark swarthy complexion, has black hair, and is supposed to have carried off with him a coat of a light blue and white mixture, in which probably he is now dressed.

Hereford, March 25. This Day Will. Summers and Tipping were executed here for House-breaking: They behaved in a very penitent Manner, but made no Confession. At the Tree the Hangman was intoxicated with Liquor, and supposing there were three ordered for Execution, was going to put one of the Ropes about the Parson's Neck as he stood in the Cart, and was with much Difficulty prevented by the Jailer from so doing.

The Derby Mercury, 6 April 1738.

Staffmans House
(front)

The hangman's house in Stirling (from *Old Nooks of Stirling*, 1898, by J. S. Fleming).

At the execution of the rioters upon the late special commission at Gloucester, Harris, the common hangman, being at that time in gaol as a party concerned in those outrages, one Evans, of Hampton, was procured to officiate in his stead. This fellow, last week, committed some trifling theft, for which the justices ordered him to be whipped by his brother hangman, Mr. Harris, who told the delinquent that he should severely smart for the reflection he had brought upon the honourable calling to which he had been initiated, and accordingly gave him such a trimming with the cat o' nine tails as must have convinced him that the principles of honour and honesty are essential to that respectable profession.

From *Sarah Farley's Bristol Journal* of 2 May 1767 (as quoted in *Gloucestershire Notes and Queries*, IV, 266-7).

The former hangman apparently remained at large for several weeks after the publication of this notice and, in fact, was never tried in connection with any of the offences committed in Edinburgh. He was, however, tried in Stirling on 12 May of that year for stealing a pair of sheets and two shirts in Airth, in the same county, in March. He was convicted and sentenced to transportation for life.

The £5 reward which had been offered for his capture was paid to a man named John Clark, of whom nothing more is known.

* * *

On 2 February 1771, John Rankine, the Stirling hangman, was removed from office, following various complaints about his conduct. The Stirling Town Council Minutes for that date tell us that he had at times been unable to perform his duties and also that he and his wife kept 'a Bad house in the Night time by entertaining Tinkers and Vagabonds & having quarrels with them to the great nuisance & disturbance of the Neighbourhood'. They go on to say that after depriving Rankine of his livelihood, the Council instructed the Burgh Treasurer to give him ten shillings 'for paying the Expence of Carrying him & his Wife to Glasgow or elsewhere'.

Rankine was the last known hangman of Stirling. It is not known how long he had held the post or what became of him following his dismissal.

Stirling continued to have a hangman of its own only until 1790, thereafter using the services of hangmen from other towns whenever there was an execution to be carried out there. The last reference in the Burgh Accounts to a local hangman is an entry recording a payment of £4 19s 'for Staffman from 1 Nov. 1789 to 17 May 1790'.

On the 19th of September, Capt. Crosby, who deserted from the British army in Flanders, and came to Scotland with the French troops, was hanged, and two other deserters shot, at Perth. The hangman of Perth absconded on this occasion; and one called from Stirling, died on the road. Thereupon a prisoner brought out of jail officiated.

The Scots Magazine, 1746, pp. 445-6.

* * *

At the Somerset Assizes held in Bridgwater early in August 1785, Thomas Woodham, the sixty-nine-year-old hangman of Gloucestershire, was sentenced to death for highway robbery.

Woodham had robbed a man named William Wiltshire of 1s 6d near the village of Batheaston. The date of the crime does not appear in any of the surviving records, but the culprit was evidently still at liberty on 18 July, when he is known to have carried out a hanging in Gloucester.

Woodham was not reprieved or pardoned and, with five other offenders, was himself hanged in Ilchester on 10 August. On his way to the gallows, he expressed regret at not having been able to hang two or three other prisoners who were still awaiting execution in his own county.

The six condemned were all hanged together from the back of a cart, but three of them had to be hanged a second time, the ropes having slipped from their necks at the first attempt. Woodham was not one of those who suffered this additional ordeal.

In its account of the execution, the *General Evening Post* says that Woodham had also been tried several times in Gloucester. Unfortunately, it does not give any details of the trials and none have been discovered elsewhere.

* * *

In March 1769, at the Court of Great Sessions for the County of Flint, one Edward Edwards was sentenced to death for burglary. The county, however, had no regular hangman, and when Edwards was left for execution the Deputy Sheriff, Ralph Griffith, feared that it would be virtually impossible for him to find any native of Wales willing to carry out the sentence. He therefore had inquiries made in Liverpool and Shrewsbury in the hope of finding an Englishman willing to act as executioner.

Before long, a man in Shropshire agreed to perform the hanging and was given five guineas in part payment for this service. He then set out for Wales in company with two other men who had been hired to escort him, but deserted his companions on the road, taking the five guineas with him. The two escorts searched for the man in vain and then tried to find somebody else to serve as hangman in his place - also without success.

Eventually, John Babington, a prisoner in the same jail as Edwards, agreed to undertake the task. The execution thus took place in June, some two months after the date on which it was originally to have been carried out.

For acting as hangman, Babington was paid six guineas, and for persuading him to do it, his wife was paid another six. Ralph Griffith afterwards calculated the expenses which had been incurred by his clerks, his messengers, his agents and himself in connection with the affair as follows:

Travelling and other expenses:	£15	10s	0d
Payment to Shropshire man:	£5	5s	0d
Cost and expenses of escorts:	£4	10s	0d
To Babington:	£6	6s	0d
To Babington's wife:	£6	6s	0d
Materials and labour for gallows:	£4	12s	0d
Cart, coffin and burial:	£2	10s	0d
Additional expenses (minimum):	£5	0s	0d
Total:	£49	19s	0d

Another case in which a county in Wales had difficulty finding a hangman was that of David Williams, a prisoner under sentence of death in Merioneth in 1743. Williams *was* hanged by an Englishman who had been brought over to Wales especially for the purpose, but there appears to be no record of how much that execution cost the authority concerned.

In a third case, in Anglesey in 1745, the procurement of an executioner and the erection of a pillory were together estimated to have cost £60.

11. Brunskill and His Mate

On 22 November 1786, the new London hangman, William Brunskill, had seven people to hang outside the Debtors' Door of Newgate Prison. He apparently dispatched them without mishap, but his behaviour after the platform fell was most unusual. 'It is a fact,' says the *Daily Universal Register* of 27 November,

> that at the execution on Wednesday morning, the successor to the late Jack Ketch, when the operation was over, turned round to the populace, and making a profound bow seemed to enquire how they approved his first performance?

It was an improper way to behave on such an occasion, and Brunskill may well have been taken to task by the sheriffs over it. However, he kept his position and went on to become the longest-serving hangman of London since Gregory Brandon.

At the time of his appointment, Brunskill was about forty-three years of age. He had served as his predecessor's deputy or assistant for at least twelve years and had officiated at hangings himself in 1780, while Dennis was in jail.

It is not known who Brunskill had to assist *him* during his early years as hangman, but about 1790 he took on John Langley, a labourer aged about twenty-four, who was to continue working with him for the rest of his long career.

Brunskill's first year or so in office must have been quite lucrative, for in 1787 ninety-two people were executed in London alone: the second highest annual total for several decades. But in subsequent years the number was much lower, averaging twenty-eight a year between 1788 and 1792, and falling to just sixteen in 1793. Brunskill was thus plunged into poverty.

In January 1794, he petitioned the Court of Aldermen for relief. His petition stated that he was obliged to keep an assistant, 'though his allowance was so small and his income so trifling, as to be insufficient to maintain himself and family'. The Court referred the matter to the sheriffs.

Either then or at some later stage, the sheriffs began to pay Brunskill wages of one guinea a week in place of the quarterly salary which he had previously received. At first, he still had to pay an allowance to his assistant, but later the sheriffs began to employ Langley themselves, paying him wages of 10s 6d a week.

Among noteworthy executions carried out by Brunskill was that of Christian Murphy, the last woman to be burnt at the stake in England. Mrs Murphy and her husband had both been convicted of coining, which at that time was treated as treason. But while women convicted of this offence were burnt, men, for some unknown reason, were merely hanged.

With seven other offenders, Mrs Murphy's husband was hanged outside Newgate Prison on the morning of 18 March 1789. Shortly afterwards, she herself was brought out of the prison and chained to a stake a few yards from the scaffold. The stake in this case had a projecting arm, from which the condemned woman was hanged for half an hour before she was burnt. The following year, judicial burning was abolished.

Brunskill's other victims included Colonel Edward Marcus Despard, who was executed with six associates at Horsemonger Lane, the county jail of Surrey, on 21 February 1803. The seven men had been sentenced to be hanged, drawn and quartered for plotting to assassinate George III, but were actually just hanged and then beheaded after death.

As was usual at Horsemonger Lane, this execution took place on a scaffold on the prison roof. The decapitation of the corpses was performed, not by Brunskill, but by a masked man who was rumoured to be a surgeon. In keeping with tradition, however, Brunskill held up each head as it was cut off, calling out to the crowds, 'This is the head of a traitor!'

At a double hanging at Newgate in 1797, an accident occurred. The two condemned, Martin Clench and James Mackley, were standing with the ropes round their necks when the platform suddenly gave way. Brunskill, Langley and two clergymen who had been attending the prisoners all fell to the ground, while Clench and Mackley were hanged with their faces uncovered. One of the clergymen was badly hurt.

The drops given at these early Newgate hangings were not very long. The bodies of the condemned could still be seen after the platform had fallen, though their legs were partially concealed by the sides of the scaffold. As the condemned rarely died instantly, it had become the practice for the hangman or his assistant (or both) to go underneath the scaffold and pull their legs.

In 1802, Joseph Wall, a former Governor of the island of Goree, near Cape Verde (Senegal), was hanged for the murder of a soldier named Armstrong, who had died twenty years earlier as a result of being flogged on his orders. Wall had, inexplicably, objected to the idea of his legs being pulled and had obtained a promise that they would not be. But after he had been hanging for a quarter of an hour, he was still alive and in convulsions; Brunskill and his mate then acted against his wishes and pulled his legs until he was dead.

On 22 August 1814, Brunskill had six people to hang, one of whom was a

---

At the execution of three offenders at Newgate in 1807, the pressure of the crowd was so great that some people fell over and others fell on top of them. In the struggle that ensued, panic broke out and thirty people were trampled to death. Fifteen others were injured.

A Newgate execution in 1809 (from a contemporary print).

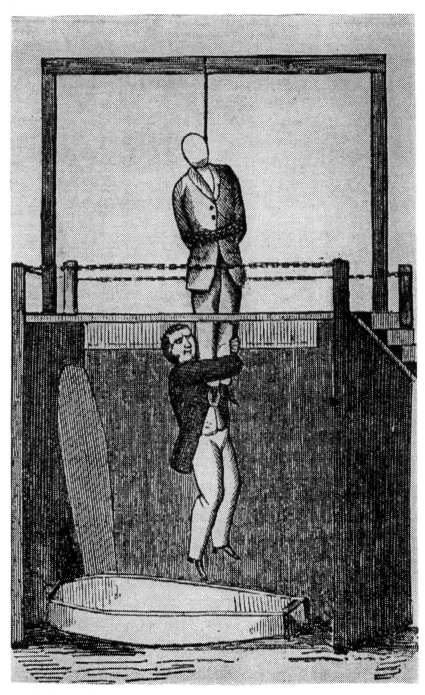

A nineteenth-century picture of an execution at Newgate, with the
hangman, unseen by the spectators, pulling the legs of the condemned.

robber named John Ashton. Ashton, who was apparently insane, danced on the scaffold, exclaiming repeatedly, 'I'm Lord Wellington!' When the platform fell, an extraordinary thing happened: Ashton rebounded from the rope and landed back on the floor of the scaffold, where he started dancing again. 'What do ye think of me?' he called out to the spectators. 'Am I not Lord Wellington now?' Brunskill then had to go back onto the scaffold and push him off.

About three months after Ashton's execution, Brunskill suffered a stroke. Though this left him quite incapable of work, he was allowed to retain the post of hangman for several months longer, with John Langley performing his duties for him. One James Botting was engaged as Langley's assistant, and was paid the usual 10s 6d a week by the sheriffs.

In May 1815, at the age of seventy-two, Brunskill petitioned the Court of Aldermen, informing them that he wished to resign from his post on account of his incapacity. The petition, read on 9 May, stated that he had 'served the Office of Executioner upwards of forty years' and asked for financial support in his retirement. The Court was sympathetic and granted him a pension of 15s a week. What became of him afterwards is unknown.

Langley went on serving as hangman for the next two years, but then became ill himself and died at the London Hospital on 27 April 1817. Reporting his death, *Bell's Weekly Messenger* of 4 May said that he had been an out-patient at the hospital for some time prior to his admission. The Record Book of the hospital

EXECUTION - On Thursday morning at nine o'clock the four Malays, Caedan, Panjang, Moodie, and Sootoo, were removed from Newgate for execution in the following procession: - A party of the Horse Patrol, to clear the way, Constables about 100 four abreast, City Marshall, on horseback, the two Sheriffs, in their carriages, constables, the Cart, in which the culprits sat on two seats, their faces towards the horses; they were pinioned, and the halter round each of their necks; the two hangmen, one on each side in the cart, each with a cutlass, and two interpreters. The culprits were dressed like English sailors, and wore striped woollen caps. The procession passed along Newgate-street, Cheapside, Whitechapel, the Commercial-road, to Execution Dock, where there was a temporary gallows erected at low water mark, and at ten o'clock they were launched into eternity. At eleven o'clock, they were cut down and lowered into a boat, and their bodies given to the surgeons for dissection.

A *Bell's Weekly Messenger* report of the execution of four Malay seamen for a murder committed on the high seas. The report was published on 18 December 1814.

A multiple hanging at Horsemonger Lane Jail (from William Jackson's *New and Complete Newgate Calendar*, 1818).

A double hanging on Shooter's Hill, near Woolwich, in 1809 (from an old print).

gives the cause of his death merely as 'mortification'.

Langley, who was fifty-one years old, left a wife and three children: the eldest child was aged eleven, the youngest just ten months. Shortly after his death, his widow, Elizabeth, having no means of support, petitioned the Court of Aldermen for assistance, but was not treated at all generously.

The Court merely resolved (somewhat confusingly, in view of the fact that John Langley had been paid weekly) 'that the Sheriffs be recommended to pay the said Elizabeth Langley the Salary which would have been due to her Husband at Midsummer next'.

12. Old Ned

Edward Barlow, commonly called 'Old Ned', was hangman of Lancashire for thirty-one years. Born in 1736, he was appointed to the post about 1781, and remained in it until his death in 1812. An obituary notice in a Manchester newspaper describes him as 'one of the greatest terrors to vice ever known in this part of the kingdom'; a brief character sketch published in 1843, however, portrays him as a repulsive fellow, much despised in his own community.

'It is said he was equally as great a villain as any man he ever put to death,' says Joseph Hall, in a short book entitled *Lancaster Castle; its History and Associations*.

> He was guilty of nearly every vile act; was many times convicted, and twice sentenced to transportation for life. He often used to boast he had 'rid the world of many a rogue, and saved the life of one honest man;' he having, on one occasion, rescued a very worthy individual from a watery grave.

Hall gives us no details of Barlow's alleged crimes and makes no further mention of the person he is said to have rescued. Of the way in which the hangman was treated by others, he has this to say:

> From information we learn that this man led a wretched life; there were very few houses into which he was permitted to enter; he was ever the butt of scorn for all persons; many times he was seriously abused; often pelted with missiles of the foulest description; and not unfrequently was he rolled in the mud, and as often much worse treated in a nameless manner(.)

The sketch is actually not very accurate. For one thing, it claims that Barlow officiated at a multiple hanging in 1817, Hall having failed to discover that he had died five years earlier. It also appears from the few known references to Barlow in contemporary newspapers that he was *not* 'many times' convicted of criminal offences and may well have been convicted only once. No doubt some of the other claims made by Hall are exaggerations, too.

Barlow is said to have been a Welshman, but his birthplace is unknown. During his thirty-one years as hangman, he carried out death sentences on 131 offenders, many of them at Lancaster Castle and others on Lancaster Common (last used for an execution in 1799). The 'new drop', on which seven people were hanged together after the March Assizes of 1801, stood just outside the Castle, on a site now called the Hanging Corner.

The 'wretched life' Old Ned is said to have led could not have been as bad as

Saturday last the undernamed seven unfortunate fellow-men were launched into eternity, at Lancaster, from the New-drop at the prison of that town: Charles Moore, John Moore, (brothers), J. Wilkinson, William Ryder, Charles Fowles, John Lee alias Thompson, Michael Brady alias McGunnis. - They met death with astonishing resignation and fortitude.

The Manchester Gazette and Weekly Advertiser, 2 May 1801.

Hall would have us believe, for he does not seem to have lived in fear or been at all ashamed of his occupation. 'His profession (strange to tell) was to him a subject of pride and boasting, and he would talk of the neatness in which he would execute it,' says his obituary in *Cowdroy's Manchester Gazette.*

The one time that Barlow is known to have been convicted of a criminal offence was in 1806, when he was tried at Lancaster's March Assizes for stealing a horse. The horse in question was a chestnut-coloured gelding belonging to a Peter Wright, of North Meols, near Southport, and the hangman had been committed for trial on 28 December previously. The *Morning Post* of 11 April reported that on leaving the dock after being found guilty, he exclaimed, 'All this comes of a man getting out of his line!'

Barlow was sentenced to death, but his sentence was commuted to ten years' imprisonment, to be served in Lancaster Castle. He was sixty-nine years old at that time and had been hangman for about twenty-five years.

Despite being a prisoner, he was allowed to retain his official post, and carried out many more hangings over the course of the next six and a half years. The conditions of his confinement are unknown, but he was obviously kept apart from the other prisoners, for his own protection.

Old Ned died, at the age of seventy-six, on 9 December 1812, and was buried the following day at St Mary's Church, Lancaster, just a stone's-throw from the Hanging Corner. He was still a prisoner at his death: a fact which was noted in his burial entry.

Nobody seems to have been appointed to succeed him as hangman of Lancashire. With his passing, the authorities of that county must therefore have started using the services of executioners from elsewhere.

13. A Man from the Hulks

While Edward Barlow was a prisoner in Lancaster Castle, his brother functionary in Yorkshire was a prisoner in York Castle. This, in itself, is not remarkable, as the York hangman was by tradition a pardoned capital offender. This particular one, however, was unusual in that he had been under sentence of death twice.

William Curry, often erroneously called John Curry, had been condemned for the first time at the York Assizes in March 1793, after pleading guilty to a charge of stealing three sheep, together worth £3. The crime had taken place on 13 December previously, in the township of Romanby, near Northallerton, in what was then the North Riding. The sheep were the property of William Smith, a Northallerton innkeeper.

Curry, also known as William Wilkinson, lived in Thirsk, eight miles to the south-east of Northallerton. Described as a labourer, he had actually been charged with three separate offences, all of a similar nature, but was not tried for either of the others. The death sentence passed on him on this occasion was commuted to seven years' transportation.

Transportation, by this time, was to Australia, the sending of offenders to America having ended with the Declaration of Independence in 1776. But many convicts with sentences of this type (particularly those whose terms were seven years or less) were not now sent abroad at all: they served their sentences with hard labour in England instead. And this is what happened in Curry's case.

Curry served *his* sentence on the prison hulks at Woolwich. When he had completed it, he returned to Yorkshire, but within five months of his release he was in trouble again. On 18 August 1800, the *York Courant* reported:

> Last week was committed to the Castle, William Currey, otherwise Wilkinson, charged upon oath with stealing five ewe sheep, the property of Tho. Severs of this City. - N.B. The above person was convicted at this Castle, in March 1793, of a similar offence, and has since served 7 years on the Hulks at Woolwich, and was discharged therefrom the 18th of March last.

Curry duly appeared for trial again at the March Assizes the following year. Now said to be thirty-one years of age (though he may actually have been up to five years older), he again pleaded guilty and was again sentenced to death. This time the sentence was commuted to fourteen years' transportation.

A year later he was still in York Castle, presumably waiting to be sent to Australia (or back to the hulks), when the post of hangman became vacant. Curry was offered the post and prevailed upon to accept it; as a result, he served the remainder of his sentence in the same jail, from which he was eventually released

By courtesy of the National Maritime Museum, Greenwich, London

Convicts from the prison hulks at Woolwich working ashore, about 1790 (from a contemporary engraving).

in 1814 or 1815.

As in Barlow's case, we do not know the conditions of his confinement, but may reasonably suppose that, for his own safety, he was not allowed to have much to do with his fellow prisoners.

*   *   *

William Curry was hangman of York for over thirty-three years: from the summer of 1802 until his retirement towards the end of 1835. During that time, he became a wellknown character and was commonly called 'Mutton' Curry, on account of his convictions.

He executed, in all, several dozen people in York - including fourteen who were hanged in one day in 1813 - and also travelled to other towns in the north of England where his services were required. Most of the York executions were carried out at the Castle, where a 'new drop' had been erected about the time of his appointment. It was there that he officiated for the first time on 28 August 1802, when three men were hanged together, one of them for stealing sheep.

'It is generally acknowledged,' says a report of his retirement in the *Yorkshire Gazette*, 'that he filled the situation with sufficient ability; but it is to be much regretted that, whilst preparing the final noose for his unfortunate victims, gin was apt to provide a snare to him, and that he could never be induced to adjust a hempen cord without an undue allowance of blue thread.'

This proclivity led to a shocking performance at the execution of a robber named William Brown, who was hanged in York on 14 April 1821. Curry had two separate executions to perform that day: the first, at York Castle (the County Jail), was carried out without incident shortly before midday. Brown's took place at the City Jail, at Baile Hill, a little over an hour later.

'Unfortunately for Curry Wilkinson,' says the *Gazette's* account of the hangings,

> in proceeding from the County execution which he had conducted with his usual propriety, to the place of execution for the City, he was recognised by the populace, who were posting with unsatiated appetites from one feast of death to another: by a strange inconsistency, they hustled and insulted the executioner to such a degree during the whole of his walk, that he arrived nearly exhausted; and with nerves quite inadequate to the task he had still to perform.

The report then continues: 'Under these circumstances, it was, that he unfortunately applied the stimulus of spirits, which a sterner and more relentless character would not have required. The result is too well known - his head became affected, and he exhibited a spectacle much to be regretted.'

The *Gazette* does not tell us much about what happened at the second hanging: it merely says that the hangman appeared on the platform drunk and that he 'did not go through his task with that decorum which the solemnity of the occasion required'. Other reports, however, give further details of his misconduct.

It is clear from these that Curry was indeed drunk when he arrived at the City Jail, and that while waiting on the scaffold for the condemned man he became quite jocular. Shaking the halter at the spectators, he called out to them with apparent glee, 'Some of you come up and I'll try it!'

The hanging itself was a distressing spectacle, Curry being quite unable to carry it out properly on his own. 'The executioner, in a bungling manner, and with great difficulty (being in a state of intoxication), placed the cap over the culprit's face, and attempted several times to place the rope round his neck, but was unable,' says *The Times* of 24 April.

> He missed the unfortunate man's head with the noose every time that he tried. The cap was each time removed from the malefactor's face, who stared wildly round upon the spectators.

All of this is corroborated by the *York Courant's* account, which also says that after drawing down the cap the hangman found that the rope was too short and had to adjust it.

The crowd protested at the hangman's behaviour and called out to the Under-Sheriff to intervene, but for some reason he chose not to do so. 'Mr. Ryan, the humane Governor of the gaol, much affected, advanced to the front of the drop, and entreated the populace to preserve silence, which they did immediately,' *The Times* tells us. 'The executioner, however, was not able to perform his duty, without the assistance of the gaoler and one of the Sheriff's officers.'

When the hanging was finally accomplished, the crowd turned on the hangman and subjected him to shouts of execration, with some calling out, 'Hang him! Hang Jack Ketch! He's drunk!'

'On his return home, he was repeatedly knocked down and beaten by the mob,' says the *Yorkshire Gazette.*

* * *

Just a few months after the hanging of William Brown, Curry was involved in another unpleasant incident which may also have been caused by his drinking. This took place at the Castle on 1 September the same year, when five men were hanged together.

'On Saturday last, a few minutes before 12 o'clock, the five unfortunate men left for execution at our late Assizes, were conducted from their cells to the fatal drop,' says the *Gazette* of 8 September.

> After a short time spent in prayer, in which they all most fervently joined, the ropes were adjusted, and, upon a signal being given, they were launched into eternity. None of them seemed to suffer much. By an unaccountable neglect of the executioner, in not keeping sufficiently clear of the drop, when the bolt was pulled out, he fell along with the malefactors, and received some severe bruises.

The *York Herald's* report describes the reaction of the watching crowd to this mishap as follows:

> As soon as the drop fell a man was seen to fall upon the ground; when there was a cry of 'Oh! a rope has broken!' but in a minute every fear was removed, and a shout of joy burst from the crowd on observing the man get up, who proved to be no other person than the executioner, who had incautiously stood on that part of the drop which falls, at the time he undrew the bolt.

In view of the way in which he had behaved at Brown's execution, it is hardly surprising that the crowd should have been so pleased to see Curry hurt himself. It was actually quite provocative of the local sheriff to allow him to remain in the post after such a dreadful performance.

* * *

William Knipe's *Criminal Chronology of York Castle* (1867), which gives Curry's name as John Curry, claims that he was still hangman in 1836, and that he carried out the execution of Charles Batty, a twenty-eight-year-old man convicted of attempted murder, on 2 April of that year. This is incorrect.

Knipe also states that Curry died 'soon after' that execution, but this also appears to be incorrect.

Curry is now known to have retired from his post in November 1835, to spend his last days as an inmate of the Thirsk Parish Workhouse. His retirement was reported in the *Yorkshire Gazette* of 14 November 1835, which refers to him as 'Jack Ketch alias William Curry, alias Mutton Curry'. The report mentions his second conviction for sheep-stealing (though not the first), as well as his fondness for gin.

After entering the workhouse, Curry apparently lived for another five years, for the Thirsk Burial Registers of the time contain no possible reference to him until 10 March 1841, when we find an entry for 'William Curry of Thirsk, aged 76'.

Even this may not have been the William Curry in question, for in the case of workhouse inmates the registers of that parish usually say that the deceased was of 'Thirsk Union Workhouse' rather than just 'of Thirsk'. Also, there is the age discrepancy, already referred to: an 1801 Calendar of Felons gives his age as thirty-one, which suggests that he would only have been about seventy-one in 1841.

But official records were not always written as accurately as they should have been and mistakes or discrepancies often come to light when one is compared with another. It is therefore probable that the William Curry who died in 1841 *was* the old hangman.

If it was not, then we do not know what became of him.

* * *

Curry was followed as hangman by another prisoner, whose name was not published at the time. The *York Courant,* reporting the execution of Charles Batty, said that this was the first time the new functionary had officiated. It described him as 'a convict who has been confined during the last twelve months in the Castle', adding that he had been 'induced to take upon himself this revolting occupation'.

The same newspaper, on 16 April 1840, mentioned the escape of a prisoner named Coates, who had 'lately' performed the hangman's duties. Presumably, this was the man who had been appointed to the post in 1836, as there is no reason to suppose that York had had any other new hangman in the meantime.

Coates's forename is not given in the report, but he is said to have been a burglar. If so, then he was probably James Coates, a man convicted in 1835 of larceny from a dwelling-house in Leeds. Coates, then aged thirty-three, had been sentenced to seven years' transportation. He would have been a prisoner in York Castle for at least nine months prior to the execution of Charles Batty.

What became of Coates the burglar after his escape is not known. It is, however, known that his successor as hangman was a man named Nathaniel Howard, who was *not* a prisoner. Presumably, those in authority were unable to find a prisoner willing to accept the post at that time.

14. A Guinea a Week Over the Prison Gate

James Botting became hangman of London after Langley's death in April 1817. It is not known how long he remained in the post, for official records show merely that it was somewhere between two years and just under seven years. An obituary published in the *Morning Advertiser* in 1837 suggests that he left office about 1820, but this may not be very accurate.

Botting, at any rate, is known to have been a native of Brighton. John Ackerson Erredge, in his *History of Brighthelmstone* (1862), tells us that the hangman's father, known as Jemmy Botting, owned a small property in that town, situated at the back of West Field Lodge, near the bottom of Cannon Place. He says the property was called Botting's Rookery, 'from its being the resort of tramps of the lowest order'.

Jemmy's son, an illiterate man, began serving as Langley's assistant in November 1814, earning 10s 6d a week, as Langley had done before him. In April 1815, he petitioned the Court of Aldermen for an increase in pay, claiming that 10s 6d a week was 'inadequate to his own support much less that of his family'. The petition, which was obviously drawn up professionally, gave his address as 4, Badgers Court, Harlows Rents, Shoreditch.

The Court referred the matter to the sheriffs for consideration, but no increase in wages resulted. Two years after that, on 2 May 1817, Botting carried out an execution at Newgate (the first since Langley's death) with the help of a man named Henry Small. Small afterwards petitioned the Court himself, requesting that he be appointed to fill the vacant post of assistant hangman, but the Court decided that an assistant hangman was no longer needed.

Towards the end of the following year, Botting himself petitioned the Court again, claiming, as before, that his wages were insufficient to meet the needs of his family and himself. His income, by this time, was actually well over twice what it had been in April 1815: his wages, for one thing, were now a guinea a week instead of just half a guinea and he now had fees and perquisites which he had not had as Langley's assistant. But he had recently been deprived of some of his perquisites, apparently on the orders of one of the Court's committees, and an allowance which he received for attending the Old Bailey Sessions had been reduced from 2s to 1s a day.

The lost perquisites, according to Botting's petition, were all fees which he had formerly received at executions from unofficial sources. Some were from undertakers or from friends of the condemned, presumably for the bodies they sought or for his help in connection with their removal. The only other such payments he mentioned were sums paid by people suffering from wens (usually

2s 6d) for the privilege of rubbing their bodies with the hands of some executed offender. This curious practice reflected a widespread belief that the bodies of those hanged had curative powers.

The petition made no reference to perquisites which Botting had *not* lost, or to the official fees which he received in respect of each person he hanged and each whipping he inflicted. In fact, it was cunningly worded in such a way as to give the impression that he now received little more than his ordinary wages.

The petition was referred to the Court's Committee on the State of the City Jails, which reported back on 30 March 1819, recommending that no action be taken on it. The Court approved the report and no action *was* taken - at least, not officially. But the rubbing of people afflicted with wens was soon resumed, apparently without any further objection.

Although Botting had no regular assistant, his successor, James Foxen, claimed in 1828 that he had been 'one of the Executioners at the Old Bailey' (i.e., at Newgate Prison*) for ten years. It would therefore seem that he had begun assisting Botting on a casual basis about 1818, but it is unclear how he was remunerated for his work at that time.

Both the *Morning Advertiser* obituary and Erredge put the number of people executed by Botting at 175, but while the former says that he ceased to be hangman about 1820, the latter says (quite erroneously) that he was still in the post towards the end of 1824. The *Advertiser* also tells us that he referred to the condemned as 'the parties' and that he never spoke to any of them as he went about his final preparations on the scaffold.

On 1 May 1820, Arthur Thistlewood, the leader of the so-called Cato Street Conspiracy, and four fellow revolutionaries were hanged and beheaded at Newgate for plotting to assassinate the entire British Cabinet. It is generally assumed that Botting was their executioner, but some sources name Foxen as the person who officiated on that occasion. As at the execution of Despard and his associates, the decapitation of the corpses was performed by a masked man who was not the hangman.

It is clear from both Erredge and the *Advertiser* that Botting left his post through infirmity ('in consequence of paralysis', they both say), and the records of the Court of Aldermen show that this must have been before 17 February 1824, when he was granted a pension of five shillings a week. At that time, the records show, 'James Botting the late Hangman' was in prison for debt, and in addition to providing him with a pension, the Court instructed the City Solicitor to secure his release. The entry in question says nothing to indicate that he had only *just* left the post and nothing to contradict the *Advertiser's* claim that he had left it about

---

* Newgate Prison stood at the end of the street called the Old Bailey, on the site of what is now the Central Criminal Court. The Old Bailey Sessions House was next door to it.

The execution of the Cato Street Conspirators (from an old print).

> Just before the bodies were cut down, another proof was given that popular
> superstition of the most senseless kind is not yet extinct. Four females ascended
> the platform and rubbed their faces and necks with the hands of Patmore and
> Thomson. This, it is thought, is a cure for wens.
>
> From a report of a Newgate execution (*The Times*, 26 September 1821).

1820.

James Foxen, who was also illiterate, was generally called Foxton in the
newspapers. We know from a petition which *he* submitted to the Court of
Aldermen that his address in May 1828 was 19, Booth Street, Hoxton. The
petition gives his age as '60 and upwards', so he must already have been in his
fifties when he became hangman.

Foxen, like Botting, hanged many people at Newgate, and others in provincial
towns which had no hangman of their own. For his London and Middlesex
executions, he was regularly assisted by a man named Thomas Cheshire, who had
occasionally assisted Botting before him. Throughout the time he was in office,
Foxen received his wages of a guinea a week over the gate of Newgate Prison: a
custom which had been started in Botting's time, 'in conformity', it was said,
'with the feelings of the turnkeys'. It is not known how Cheshire was paid.

Foxen's victims included Charles White, a twenty-three-year-old Holborn
bookseller hanged for arson in 1827. White was executed at Newgate with one
other offender: a woman who had been sentenced to death for stealing goods from
her employer. At his own request, his arms were bound with two silk handkerchiefs instead of the usual piece of cord.

After Foxen and Cheshire had finished tying him up in readiness for his final
ordeal, White managed to get his arms free and threw off his white cap. Two
sheriff's officers immediately pinioned him afresh, but he struggled so violently
that they could not get the cap back onto his head and left him to be hanged with
his face uncovered.

By the time the signal was given for the hanging to take place, White had got
his arms free again, and as the drop fell he suddenly leapt from it and gained a
foothold on the platform of the scaffold. Clinging with both hands to the rope
above his head, he then hung there obliquely until the hangman forced him from
the platform. Even then, he struggled convulsively until his legs were pulled, his
distorted features presenting a further shocking sight to the watching crowds.

Another of the criminals executed by Foxen was William Corder, a notorious
murderer hanged in Bury St Edmunds, Suffolk, in August 1828. In this case, the
condemned gave him no trouble, but Foxen was put out by a suggestion from one

The execution of William Corder (from an old print).

of the other officials on the scaffold that he wasn't doing his job properly. The incident is described in a contemporary account by somebody named Curtis as follows:

> After the executioner had fixed the rope to the beam, and was busy in tying what he calls the 'mysterious knot,' it was suggested to him that he had left too much for what is technically called 'the fall,' in consequence of which he reluctantly took part of it up, and it was quite evident that Mister Ketch did not relish this interference with his public functions.

Foxen, in fact, was so disconcerted by it that he released the drop before the signal was given.

'After the execution was over,' says Curtis, 'Foxton expressed his chagrin at having been interrupted in the performance of his professional duty. He said, "I never like to be meddled with, because I always study the subjects which come under my hands, and, according as they are tall or short, heavy or light, I accommodate them with the fall. No man in England has had so much experience as me, or knows how to do his duty better."'

And the author adds:

> In the after part of the day, this public functionary visited the corpse in the Shire Hall, for the purpose of claiming Corder's trowsers, when he pointed to his handywork upon the neck of the criminal, and asked, exultingly, whether he had not 'done the job in a masterly manner.'

Three months before Corder's execution, in his petition to the Court of Aldermen, Foxen had claimed that he was now too old and in too poor a state of health to go on performing his duties, and had asked the Court to provide him with a pension - 'as the former Executioners have had' - so that he could retire. Yet he carried out this execution willingly enough (he was under no obligation to do so) and there is nothing in Curtis's account to bear out his claim about the state of his health.

Foxen, at any rate, was *not* granted a pension, and went on serving as hangman until his death. This took place on 14 February the following year and was reported in a number of newspapers. Some of his obituaries stated, quite incorrectly, that he had been London's 'chief executioner' for sixteen years.

Foxen was succeeded by Thomas Cheshire - sometimes called 'Jack' Cheshire - who was already a wellknown figure. But it appears that there were doubts about Cheshire's reliability, for within a few weeks another new hangman of London was appointed. This was a young man named William Calcraft, whose career as an executioner was to last for no less than forty-five years.

Cheshire was nonetheless kept on as a hangman, too, until his death in July

The execution of John Thurtell, a murderer, at Hertford Jail in 1824, carried out by Thomas Cheshire (from an old print).

During the three years ending December 1821, the total number of London and Middlesex prisoners executed was ninety-eight. During the three years 1822-4, the number was fifty-one; during the three years 1825-7, it was fifty-three, and during the three years 1828-30, it was fifty-two.

Information taken from *The Times* of 24 February 1842.

1830, apparently doing little to justify his retention. He was probably just kept on nominally, in recognition of his years of service as Foxen's assistant.

Cheshire was a married man, living in Bell Court, Giltspur Street, just a short distance from Newgate Prison. His wife was a drunkard with a tendency to violence, which got her into trouble with the law on at least one occasion. The *Times* of 20 August 1829 gives the following details of an appearance she had made at the Guildhall Magistrates Court the previous day:

Ann Cheshire, the wife of the common hangman, was brought up for re-examination, charged with assaulting four children.

A poor woman named Cahill, who lodges in the same house with the prisoner, in a court in Giltspur-street, had complained that the prisoner came home drunk on Saturday afternoon, and after knocking two of her children down while they were playing in the court, picked them up and threw them down an area into a cellar ten feet deep, and then flung two other children upon them. Neither of the four, however, were seriously hurt, and as the prisoner had suffered 40 hours' imprisonment, the complainant did not wish to press any charge.

Mr. Alderman ANSLEY said, this was such an outrageous act, that he could not allow it to be passed over in that way, and he remanded the prisoner for 48 hours more, that she might have some punishment, and that the mother of the other children might come forward to complain, if she chose.

Yesterday, when the prisoner was brought up, Mrs. Cahill was in the same forgiving temper.

Old Mr. Cheshire, assuming an over-kind good-natured manner, assured the Alderman she was remarkably attached to children, and gave them many halfpence, and it was because she had no halfpence to give them on Saturday, and they therefore bawled after her 'Jack Ketch,' that she became irritated, and accidentally knocked them down the cellar.

Notwithstanding her protestations, the alderman would not part with her until she had given sureties for her future good behaviour.

On 13 July the following year, the same newspaper reported that 'Jack Cheshire, one of the public executioners for the metropolis', had died at his lodgings in Bell Court a few days earlier. His last days, it seems, had been spent in fear of body-snatchers.

'Cheshire always had the greatest terror of the resurrection-men, and was often told, by those of that class who at last fell within his clutches, that the "trade" would have him at any risk when his mortal career should be terminated,' says the report.

> His last words were upon this subject. He requested that his blessing might be given to Mr. Wontner, the Governor of Newgate, and that gentleman's family, accompanied by the solemn entreaty that his remains should be buried in Newgate. It has, however, been thought proper to give him 'Christian burial,' and that St. Sepulchre's churchyard shall receive the body of the most ingenius of execution-ers.

'His wife, in the apprehension that an attempt would be made to steal the corpse, actually slept with her head upon the cold arm of the deceased, and on Friday night she was awakened by the noise of some of the "snatchers," who attempted to gain an entrance at the two-pair of stairs window,' the report adds.

The description of Cheshire as 'the most ingenius of executioners' is clearly an exaggeration. He had undoubtedly carried out *some* hangings himself over the years, but most of his appearances on the scaffold had been in a lesser role. The *Times* report nonetheless goes on to call him 'one of the most expert of men at the dreadful trade', claiming that the Cato Street Conspirators had been among his victims. It concludes with an allegation about his conduct which is also unlikely to have been more than partially true:

> When Cheshire officiated at Horsemonger-lane Gaol, he was obliged to perform the whole ceremony, and the manner in which he performed part of it was truly appalling. After the bolt is pulled, it is usual for the functionary to take hold of the body, in order to render the passage to the other world as quick as possible. Cheshire, the moment the pangs became visible, made a rush at the malefactor, and swung for some minutes with him, as if a certain delight were communicated by the idea of ushering a soul into eternity.

James Botting, by this time, was no longer living in Shoreditch. By March 1830 at the latest, he had gone back to live in Brighton, where he was to remain for the rest of his life. He was apparently on his own now and so disabled that he had difficulty getting about.

He overcame the problem to some extent by taking a chair each time he left his lodgings, and using it as a crutch as well as a seat as he made his way through the streets. He was thus, for some years, a familiar sight in Brighton, but few people wanted to be associated with him. Eventually, he became so feeble and nervous that he was hardly able to cross the floor of his room.

Early in October 1837, a letter arrived at London's Guildhall, informing the officials there that the ex-hangman had died. The letter was from Botting's landlord and landlady, who requested that, as he had died poor, the Corporation would be so good as to grant them 'the price of a shell and prayers for their departed brother'. The Police Committee considered the request and directed that the couple be sent £2.

In spite of the length of time which had elapsed since his retirement, Botting, during his last months, had been much preoccupied with his former profession. The impending execution of a murderer named James Greenacre, in May of that year, was of particular interest to him, and as the clock struck eight on the morning of the execution, Botting called out from his bed, 'That's the time o' day! I'm blessed if he ain't a-coming out to nap it!'

Nearer the end, his sleep was disturbed (according to his *Morning Advertiser* obituary) by 'visions of certain scenes in which he had performed a prominent character'. He used to dream that 175 'parties', with their nightcaps on and their heads inclined towards their left shoulders, were moving before him, says the *Advertiser.*

At his death, on 1 October, however, he was apparently quite calm. The *Advertiser* quotes his landlady as saying that he 'went off without saying a word, and so nobody never said a word to him'.

15. Neither a Samson nor a Hercules

On 16 April 1803, an advertisement for a hangman was published in the *Glasgow Courier*. It read as follows:

> Wanted, for the City of Glasgow, an Executioner. The bad character of the person who last held the office having brought on it a degree of discredit which it by no means deserves, the Magistrates are determined to accept of none but a sober well-behaved man. The emoluments are considerable.
>
> Applications will be received by the Lord Provost, or either of the Town Clerks.

Before long, the post was filled, apparently by a man called Archibald McArthur, who was to be hangman of Glasgow for the next ten years. It is unclear whether that really *was* his name, for a bill presented to the authorities in Ayr in respect of an execution which he carried out for them in May 1809 suggests that it may have been Archibald McLauchlane. It is, at any rate, given as McArthur in an article published in the *Glasgow Herald* in 1856, which also gives a few details of his character and career.

'This new hangman was called Archibald McArthur, or "Buffy," by which nickname he was known, in consequence of his personal appearance,' says the article.

> When made finisher of the law, he was about 30 years old, and about 5 feet 2 inches in height, stout and rotund in body, with short bandy-legs, and a big bullet-shaped head, with a florid bloated countenance, and thick lips, but was a good natured inoffensive creature. He never assumed the full dress or official costume which at times had been seen on his predecessor 'Jock Sutherland.'

At the time of his appointment, 'Buffy' was given a small cottage in South Montrose Street to live in, but attacks by mobs eventually forced him to move. He then went to live in a house in Kirk or Upper High Street, where he went on living until his last illness. He died in the Glasgow Infirmary, aged about forty.

Buffy was a married man. His wife, according to the *Herald* article, was 'a small creature, and an inveterate tippler'. Their only child was a hunchbacked boy who died before his father, in the same hospital.

The next known Glasgow hangman, Thomas Young, was the last to hold an official post in the city. He was appointed on 10 December 1814, and remained in office until his death twenty-three years later. It is not known how long the post had been vacant prior to his appointment.

Young was a native of Berwickshire and had served as a soldier in the

Berwickshire Regiment of Volunteers. He afterwards settled in Glasgow, where he worked for a while as a labourer.

During a period of unemployment, he heard that the city needed a hangman and applied for the post himself. In support of his application, he was able to produce a number of character references, including one from his late colonel. As a result, he obtained the post.

Following his appointment, Young signed an indenture, binding him to continue serving as hangman for the rest of his life. His duties, as set out in this document, included 'whipping Criminals, putting them in the pillory, or in the Stocks, or exposing them upon the platform'. He also had to work as a labourer at the New Jail, under the direction of the Superintendent of Works,

> carrying coals, putting on fires, Cleaning pavements on the out & insides of the Jail and Wards thereof and doing any other such Work about the premises as the said Superintendent may from time to time direct.

And in addition to performing these duties, Young was bound to live quietly, soberly and 'regularly in all respects'.

In return for his services, the magistrates had to pay Young a salary of £50 a year (30s every other Friday and the amount outstanding every 10 June and 10 December), and a fee of one guinea for each execution he carried out. They also had to provide him with a free house within the prison grounds, together with coal and candles, and a pair of shoes twice a year - 'it being understood that the said Thomas Young shall provide all his other Cloths, at his own expence'.

During his twenty-three years as hangman, Young executed over seventy people, fifty-six of them in Glasgow and others in Greenock, Paisley, Ayr, Stirling and possibly Dumfries. In McArthur's time, hangings in Glasgow had taken place at the Jail at the Cross, where twenty-two offenders in all are known to have been executed between 1788 and 1813. Thereafter, they were carried out at the front of the New Jail, near Glasgow Green.

The scaffold used at the New Jail was a portable one. Executions took place there in the afternoon, but the gallows was assembled the night before. Sometimes there was already a crowd at the scene by this time, as we see from a newspaper report of a hanging carried out in November 1819:

> Tuesday night shortly after eleven, the materials of the scaffold were brought in front of the gaol, and the gallows erected. It was a fine moon-light night, and there was a very considerable concourse of people present; all was still, save the dull sound of the hammer and the occasional directions uttered by the workmen to each other. Perhaps the greater part of the crowd consisted of females, and a number of them very well dressed.

By courtesy of Glasgow Museums: The People's Palace

The New Jail, Glasgow, in the 1830s (drawn and engraved by Joseph Swan).

> Elizabeth Waldrun, a miserable woman, apprehended for contravening sentence of banishment, and confined in a lock-up room, on the north side of the jail, in Glasgow, on Monday afternoon attempted to destroy herself by strangulation. She tied a napkin round the stancheon of her cell for that purpose; but fortunately being perceived by Docherty, the young man recently respited from sentence of death for robbery, an alarm was given, when the hangman, who was at hand, cut her down, and assistance being speedily procured the woman recovered.
>
> *The Edinburgh Evening Courant*, 2 November 1816.

Earlier the same year, when Alexander Robertson was hanged for robbing a warehouse, an unusually long drop was used. 'The unhappy prisoner Robertson mounted the scaffold with a firm step and a calm countenance,' says *The Times* of 13 April.

> The drop was very considerable, and the crash excited a strong sensation throughout the surrounding multitude, not less, it is supposed, than 30,000; but it was his own request, as, from his being a light man, he was afraid of struggling.

On 30 August 1820, at the same prison, a man named Wilson was executed for treason, the hangman carrying out only the first part of the sentence and a man in a mask the second. 'While (the prisoner was) hanging, blood appeared at his ears through the cap,' the *Gentleman's Magazine* recorded.

> At half-past three he was taken down, and the head was cut off, the body lying on the coffin. The man in the mask was saluted by hisses and cries of 'Murder!' The head was cut off at one blow, and held up as usual.

In 1816, Young assisted and instructed the newly-appointed hangman of Edinburgh, John Simpson, at the execution of a robber named John Black. And in 1819, he carried out an execution in Edinburgh himself after Simpson had been dismissed from office for incompetence (see Chapter 16).

A few days after Wilson's execution in Glasgow, there was a double hanging-and-beheading in Stirling, with Young again officiating as hangman and the decapitations being performed by a masked man whose identity is unknown. This was the last execution of its type to take place anywhere in Britain.

Young is also known to have inflicted many floggings in Glasgow, most of them during the first ten years of his tenure of office and all but two of them inside the New Jail. One which he carried out in public was that of John Kean, a cotton spinner who had tried to kill a fellow worker.

Kean was flogged on a temporary scaffold outside the Glasgow Courthouse on 11 May 1825. A report in the *Edinburgh Observer* (reprinted in *The Times* of 17 May) describes the spectacle as follows:

> About 10 minutes past 12 o'clock the criminal was brought out and bound to the post, when the common executioner inflicted the punishment awarded by the law - namely, 80 stripes, a punishment certainly trifling, compared to the enormity of his offence. He seemed to take it very coolly at the outset, but towards the close the feelings of pain rather overcame his resolution. When released, his back appeared considerably lacerated.

Though the flogging was to be followed by transportation for life, the *Observer* deplored what it saw as leniency in the way in which it was carried out and suggested that Young was not a strong enough man to perform such duties properly:

> The prevailing opinion is, that the punishment was not so severe as it might have been. The executioner, indeed, seemed to do all he could, but the same nerve and knowledge which are sufficient to hang a man may be very unable to flog him, which fact, it is to be regretted, was overlooked on this occasion. Our magistrates, however, could not help themselves. They were bound by the strict letter of the sentence, and could employ no other person but the executioner, certainly neither a Samson nor a Hercules in his line.

In spite of this alleged shortcoming, however, Young (according to an obituary in the *Scots Times*) was himself 'violently assaulted and well flogged' shortly afterwards 'by a party of fellows in the Humane Society House'. He had apparently been invited to the house by his attackers, to have a glass of ginger-beer with them.

Laidlaw held the handkerchief to give the signal, but in the midst of his devotion, he seemed to have forgot it, as he had it rolled up and grasped in his hand. The executioner touched him, put him in mind that he had it, and immediately he threw it from him, and the drop fell. Laidlaw died with scarcely a struggle; Cain was more convulsed; but in a few minutes they were both dead. Their bodies, after hanging the usual time, were cut down and placed in coffins, and taken into the jail.

From a report of a double execution in Glasgow, published in *The Times* on 4 November 1823.

Unlike McArthur, Young wore his official costume for executions in Glasgow: a long blue coat with yellow buttons and a scarlet collar, a cocked hat, white stockings and shoes with buckles. His obituary tells us that when he was called upon to 'do business' in any of the surrounding towns, he claimed very high fees and 'made it part of his bargain to be driven to and from the place in a carriage, attended by a companion'.

> When such instances occurred, he was lavish in his expenditure - lived in the best style - despised common liquors - drank wine and brandy, and treated his friends liberally.

Young was married and had three children. In the mid-1820s, he had two dogs and was regularly seen walking them two or three times a day. A letter written by him in 1820 is still in existence (it is held at the Stirling Council Archives).

Though quiet and inoffensive generally, Young enjoyed talking about his work. While under the influence of drink, he was inclined to become animated and to describe in detail the means by which a hanging was carried out.

During his last years, however, he was weak from old age and could no longer be relied upon to perform his duties. At some stage, the Glasgow magistrates began to retain an unofficial hangman named John Murdoch as a standby for him.

By March 1837, Young was so debilitated that he was unable to leave his house in the New Jail. He died there on 9 November of that year, leaving his family destitute.

16. Another Place, Another Name, the Same Profession

On 23 November 1816, John Simpson, a former sailor, was appointed hangman of Edinburgh. The post had been left vacant by the death of his predecessor, John High.

Simpson, like Thomas Young, entered the profession with good character references. He carried out his first hanging, with Young's help, less than three weeks later.

'On Wednesday John Black, convicted of highway robbery, was executed, pursuant to his sentence, at the west end of the Tolbooth, Edinburgh,' says *The Times* of 17 December.

> A new executioner officiated, assisted and instructed by the Glasgow executioner. A more than ordinary concourse of spectators attended, notwithstanding a fall of snow which came on at the time.

The hanging appears to have been carried out satisfactorily. For some unknown reason, however, it was not until 5 March the following year that Simpson's appointment was confirmed.

John High, or Heich, as he was often called, had been hangman since 1778. The Town Council Minutes record a payment of £2 2s made to him in 1800 and an increase in wages which he had received in 1809. Simpson's wages were 12s a week and he was also paid an allowance of 2s a week 'for House Rent and Taxes'.

On the day that his appointment as 'Lockman to the City and Dempster to the Court of Justiciary' was finally confirmed, Simpson had to carry out the pillorying of Black's cousin, John Morris, who had been sentenced for perjury. The pillorying led to a disturbance, which was reported in detail in the *Edinburgh Evening Courant* the following day:

> After the public executioner had performed the duty of fastening the criminal to a machine (bearing no resemblance to a pillory), he took his post beside it; before he descended from the platform, much disapprobation was shown by the crowd, which was speedily followed by showers of mud, pieces of ice, sticks, stones, &c. being thrown at him (the executioner).
>
> The unoffending object of their vengeance bore this barbarous treatment with great patience, and maintained his post with astonishing fortitude, till the space, feebly attempted to be kept by the old city guard, was broke in upon.
>
> The poor fellow was then treated with the most wanton cruelty, - knocked down, - trampled on, - kicked, and struck by every hand that could reach him;

By courtesy of Edinburgh City Libraries

A double hanging in Edinburgh in 1788 (from a contemporary print).

even the audacious-looking villain, then undergoing the just sentence of the law, for a heinous crime, presumed to kick the persecuted man, when he was driven within his reach by the mob; he was also observed, early in the tumult, to kick at the face of one of the city guard.

The executioner was at length delivered from his savage persecutors by four respectable persons, who succeeded in getting him into a stair, the entrance to which they defended at imminent personal danger.

A strong body of the police arrived *after* this stage of the disgraceful scene - but their services were then of no use.

The report concludes: 'We learn this morning, that John Simpson, the executioner, remains extremely ill from the bruises he received in the above-mentioned scandalous proceeding.'

Despite this unpleasant experience, Simpson continued to hold the Edinburgh post until the end of the following year, when his bungling of an execution - the city's first since the hanging of John Black - caused an even worse disturbance.

Robert Johnston, an old offender aged twenty-two, was hanged on 30 December 1818, for a robbery committed two months earlier. As in Black's case, the hanging took place on a portable scaffold at what was now Edinburgh's common place of execution: a site in the Lawnmarket, at the head of Libberton's Wynd. Unfortunately, Simpson miscalculated the length of rope that was needed, so that when the platform was lowered the condemned man's toes went on touching it. The spectators were shocked.

A loud shout of horror, with cries of 'murder,' burst from an immense multitude assembled (says a report in the *Caledonian Mercury*), and instantly a shower of stones thrown by persons in the crowd compelled the Magistrates and peace officers to abandon their stations, and no one but the criminal remained upon the scaffold; the Magistrates, clergymen, &c. being under the necessity of retiring into the porch of the Tolbooth church, adjacent to the Writers' Library; and from thence, through the aisle of the High Church, into the Police Office.

Another cry of 'Cut him down - he is alive,' succeeded; and a person, genteelly dressed, sprung upon the platform, cut the rope, and the culprit fell down in a reclining position upon the scaffold, after having hung about five minutes.

A riot ensued. Several more people climbed onto the scaffold and took the ropes from the hanged man's neck and arms and the cap from his face. Finding that he *was* still alive, they then removed him from the scaffold and carried him off in the direction of the High Street, while other rioters went on stoning the police and attacked the hangman.

With the arrival of police reinforcements, the condemned man was retaken at the head of Advocates Close and carried into a nearby police office. There he was

The attempted rescue of Robert Johnston (from the *Life and Recollections of Calcraft the Hangman*, 1880).

attended by a surgeon, who bled him in both arms and in the temporal vein. In the meantime, soldiers from the Castle began restoring order to the streets.

Three quarters of an hour after being cut down from the gallows, Johnston was brought out to be hanged again. The surgeon had managed to revive him, but he had to be carried and couldn't speak. The Lord Provost then addressed the crowd, calling on everyone present to conduct themselves peacefully. He told them that the magistrates had a painful duty imposed on them, which they were bound, under any circumstances, to fulfil.

Though beaten by the crowd, Simpson was evidently not as badly hurt as he had been at the pillorying of John Morris: he was still able to resume his duty. But when the condemned man was hanged again, the rope was again found to be too long: this time, Johnston was lifted up so that it could be turned several times round the overhead hook to which it was attached.

'Another shout of "murder," and "shame, shame," broke from the crowd,' says the *Caledonian Mercury,*

> but the place was now well guarded with soldiers; and fortunately no farther outrage was attempted. - Johnston was observed to struggle very much; but his sufferings were at an end in a few minutes. The soldiers, who behaved throughout with the utmost propriety, remained on the spot until the body was cut down; and as it was then about dusk, the crowd gradually dispersed.

John Simpson was dismissed from his post the following morning. He afterwards left Edinburgh, probably without delay, for he must have been in considerable danger all the time he remained there. He had not been replaced as hangman by April 1819, when the city had another execution to be carried out, so the magistrates sent for Thomas Young. This time there was no bungling and no disturbance.

Simpson settled in Perth under the name of John Foster. Somehow he managed to get himself appointed hangman of that town - it is not known whether the local magistrates knew his real identity - but was never called upon to hang anyone there. He died of typhus in the town jail in late October or early November of the same year.

17. A Second Miscellany

On 19 December 1833, the Town Council of Inverness decided to dispense with the services of its hangman. Donald Ross had been the holder of that post since 1812, but during the whole of that time the town had had only three executions. It was therefore felt that it no longer needed to maintain such a functionary.

The decision was reported in the *Inverness Courier* of 25 December, which also published details of the hangman's income. Since his appointment, Ross, according to the *Courier*, had enjoyed an annual salary of £16, together with various other emoluments ('bites and nibbles at the public purse') which the report listed as follows:

First, he was provided with a house, bed, and bedding.
Second, he was allowed thirty-six peats weekly from the tacksman of the petty customs.
Third, he had a bushel of coals out of every cargo of English coals imported into the town.
Fourth, he was allowed a piece of coal, as large as he could carry, out of every cargo of Scotch coals.
Fifth, he had a peck of oatmeal out of every hundred bolls landed at the shore.
Sixth, he had a fish from every creel or basket of fish brought to the market.
Seventh, he had a penny for every sack of oatmeal sold at the market.
Eighth, he had a peck of salt out of every cargo.
Ninth, he was allowed every year a suit of clothes, two shirts, two pairs of stockings, a hat, and two pairs of shoes.
Added to these fixed and regular sources of income, (he) levied black mail on the lieges in the shape of Christmas boxes, and had besides a sum of five pounds at every execution at which he presided.

The *Courier* reckoned the hangman's post to be worth between fifty and sixty pounds a year when these 'bites and nibbles' were taken into account and said the three executions that Ross had carried out in Inverness must therefore have cost the town nearly £400 each.

In spite of all his perquisites, however, it appears that Ross was not considered to be very reliable, for the *Inverness Journal* of 21 October 1831, reporting arrangements for the execution of one Hugh Macleod, informed its readers: 'It has been deemed prudent in the mean time to imprison Donald Ross, the executioner, to prevent his absconding.'

Prior to Ross's appointment, the post of hangman of Inverness had been vacant for some time, following the death of its previous occupant, William Taylor.

Taylor had gone to Elgin on 'professional business', and had been attacked and killed by a mob on his way home. The *Journal* of 25 April 1811 contains brief details of the trial of two shoemakers' apprentices, James McCurroch and John Dawson, for 'assaulting, stabbing, and otherwise maltreating' him. Both were convicted and sentenced to seven years' transportation.

* * *

Aberdeen continued to have a hangman of its own until just one month after the dismissal of Donald Ross. Various references to individual holders of the post are to be found in the town's Council Registers and Burgh Accounts.

In 1770-1, a hangman whose name is unrecorded was paid a salary of 6s 8d a month, together with 15s a year for his house-rent and £2 14s for clothes. No doubt he had other sources of income as well, but these are not mentioned in the council records.

On 30 December 1773, Robert Welsh, newly appointed to the post, petitioned for an increase in salary and the Town Council raised it to 13s 4d a month. He was still in office in 1800-1, when his total recorded income was £12 7s, but in 1803-4 he was succeeded by John McDonald. McDonald died about the end of March 1805 and the town was then without a hangman until the appointment of John Milne a year later.

Milne, a convicted thief, had been sentenced to seven years' transportation in September 1805. Towards the end of that year, he applied for the vacant post, which the town's magistrates had been vainly trying to fill ever since McDonald's death. Before long, a pardon was procured for him and he was then appointed hangman (this was in April 1806) and paid £7 10s for his first six months' salary. Milne was still in office in 1818-19, when his total recorded income was £19.

Milne was married twice. His first wife, by whom he had eight children, died shortly before his conviction for theft. At the time of his imprisonment, Milne was described as a dyker or labourer.

The hangman of Aberdeen's salary was increased to £25 a year in 1822, and then remained unchanged until 27 January 1834, when the Town Council

---

Christian Waters or Milne, relict of the late hangman, was once more brought before the Police Court, on Wednesday, charged with committing a breach of the peace at Hangman's Brae, and breaking a pane of glass in the house of her husband's successor. She was sent 60 days to Bridewell.

Aberdeen Journal, 26 October 1831.

abolished the post.

One person hanged in Aberdeen during the time that Robert Welsh was in office was an offender named James Grant, whose execution was reported in the *Aberdeen Journal* of 1 July 1788. The report states:

> On Friday last, James Grant was hanged here in pursuance of his sentence at last circuit, for shop-breaking. He was executed in the way now used in England; a scaffold being erected in front of the prison, over which the gibbet projected; the place on which the criminal stood was made to fall down, and leave him suspended.

In John Milne's time, John Barnet, alias McBarnet, was hanged for housebreaking and theft. His execution, on 6 November 1818, was reported in the *Caledonian Mercury*, which tells us:

> He died with great struggle; and, after hanging the usual time, the body was cut down, and conveyed, under the attending escort of the 88th regiment, to a boat ready to receive it, in which it was carried out, and sunk at sea.

In 1830, there occurred the execution of Catherine Davidson, alias Humphrey, for the murder of her husband. She was the first woman to be hanged in Aberdeen for forty-five years.

The hangman on this occasion was named Scott, and was said to be the assistant to the Edinburgh hangman. In all likelihood, it was John Scott (see Chapter 18), who is known to have been employed by the town and was later to be hangman of Edinburgh himself.

*   *   *

James Aird was hangman of Ayr from December 1815 until his death in August 1823. During that time, he lived in an apartment in the old Wallace Tower, provided for him by the Ayr Town Council. His salary was £30 a year.

Aird was a solitary figure. A native of Tarbolton, in the same county, he was separated from his wife and children and kept owls, rabbits and other birds and beasts as his only companions. But he performed many services for his neighbours, such as ridding their houses of mice, without accepting anything from them in return. He seems, in fact, to have been quite a good-natured man in general.

'To his fellow-creature in poverty he opened his hand liberally, - to all he behaved with a respect and modesty seldom or perhaps never before combined with his office - and in the execution of his horrible duty he happily blended steadiness of purpose with great humanity to the suffering object,' says an obituary in the *Air Advertiser*.

> In short, he bore himself so, in his repulsive office, and in his transactions in his uncommon life, as to render himself, while living, to both old and young, to the evil-doer as well as to the good, an object of respect rather than aversion - and his death, consequently, has become a subject of regret rather than of rejoicing.

Aird's apartment in the Old Tower had been occupied by other Ayr hangmen before him - the ringing of the tower bell was one of the hangman's duties at this time - but prior to his appointment the building had been allowed to fall into a state of dilapidation. During his tenure of office, Aird himself spent a lot of time renovating it.

One day in August 1823, while aboard a ship in the local harbour, Aird was accidentally struck in the side by a handspike. The blow was a severe one and may well have been the cause of his death, though it appears from his *Advertiser* obituary that he may also have been suffering from epilepsy.

He somehow managed to get back to the tower, but there was then no sign of him in the neighbourhood for several days. On the Sunday following the accident the tower bell was silent and other town officials went to find out what had happened to him.

Breaking into the building, they found the hangman lying dead on the stairs leading up to the belfry from his apartment. Some of the animals which depended on him for sustenance were also dead.

In view of Aird's good character, the magistrates of the town decided that his wife and children should receive his full salary for the current quarter. As their whereabouts were unknown, however (they were believed to be in England), the Treasurer was instructed to pay the money to Aird's brother Hugh, a weaver in Darvel, whom they made responsible for forwarding it to them.

* * *

In 1816, the hangman of Chester was a man named Samuel Burrows. His name is mentioned in the *Lancaster Gazette* of 19 October of that year, in a paragraph reprinted from a second newspaper, challenging statements made in a third.

The contentious item claimed that a public meeting had been held in Chester 'to consider the present distresses of the country', and that a certain clergyman had addressed it, delivering a highly inflammatory speech. One of the other speakers was said to be 'Mr Samuel Burrows'.

The paragraph challenging this report states that no such meeting had taken place; that some of the people alleged to have taken part in it were 'persons who, from their situations in life, would not be permitted to participate in proceedings of such respectability', and that the clergyman mentioned had been away from Chester on the day in question. 'Mr Samuel Burrows' was cited as one of the people who would not have been allowed to take part in such proceedings.

Burrows is known to have hanged John Connor, a robber, in Ruthin in 1824. On the night before that particular execution he was almost hanged himself while demonstrating his technique in a local public-house.

On 15 September 1830, in Beaumaris, he hanged William Griffith, an offender who put up a desperate struggle and had to be dragged all the way to the gallows. Griffith, a married man, had been convicted of attempting to murder his wife. His execution, which attracted a great many spectators, took place on a scaffold projecting from the side of the prison.

*   *   *

On 2 October 1833, Robert Tennant, a convicted murderer, was hanged outside the courthouse in Stirling. The execution was carried out by John Williams, the Edinburgh hangman.

Williams had been in office only since 16 February previously and hadn't yet performed any hangings in Edinburgh.* Due to an oversight, he adjusted the rope

---

A little before ten o'clock Samuel Burrows, the Chester executioner, was admitted into the cell, and, after a desperate struggle, succeeded in pinioning the prisoner with a cord at the elbows. The reverend chaplain then commenced reading the funeral service, and the prisoner was led, or rather dragged, between two officers to the scaffold, on which the javelin men and others, whose duty required their presence, were already placed. When arrived at the scaffold, and placed under the beam, Griffith, who appears to have reserved his strength for a last struggle, made a desperate resistance to the executioner putting the halter round his neck, and even when this was accomplished he made continual efforts to displace it till the drop was withdrawn, which was done within five minutes from the time he came upon the scaffold. His death was, to all appearance, instantaneous; and after hanging for about an hour, his body was cut down, and placed in a coffin for interment, which took place in the evening.

From a report of the execution of William Griffith, published in the *Chester Courant and Anglo-Welsh Gazette* of 21 September 1830.

---

* Williams was a former soldier. He had been appointed hangman in place of his father, Thomas Williams, who had recently died.

round the condemned man's neck without taking off his neckcloth; then, when the mistake was pointed out to him, he held up the execution in order to remove it. By this time, Tennant had given the signal (the dropping of a handkerchief) for the hangman to 'launch him into Eternity' and the unexpected delay caused him to become very agitated during his last few moments. On his way home afterwards, Williams was attacked by a mob.

'As the executioner was proceeding through the Castlehill, on his return to Edinburgh, a crowd followed him till he reached some gardens near the bridge, in one of which he took shelter to escape the vengeance of the mob, who had become outrageous,' says a report in *The Times*.

> They pursued him into the garden, where they got hold of him, and struck and abused him. Seeing his life in imminent peril, he made a desperate effort to escape, and ran towards the river, followed by the crowd, who showered stones after him, several of which struck him.
>
> On reaching the river he plunged in, and swam towards the opposite side, where he was in great danger till the high constables arrived and drove off the crowd, and conveyed him to the gaol for safety.

The bungling of Tennant's execution did not prevent John Williams from being engaged to carry out a hanging in Greenlaw six months later - and that one apparently took place without incident. The next time he officiated on the scaffold, however, he was quite unable to perform his duty properly, probably because he was under the influence of drink.

This third execution of Williams's career was that of James Bell, a murderer hanged in Edinburgh on 13 July 1835. Bell, a twenty-six-year-old man of previous good character, had allegedly suffered harsh treatment at the hands of his victim, a Sergeant Major Moorhead, but was nonetheless piously resigned to the fate which awaited him. His hanging was attended by a great many people.

On going to pinion him just before the procession to the gallows began, Williams started crying and had difficulty accomplishing even that task. On the scaffold, according to a report in the *Edinburgh Evening Courant*, he 'made one or two awkward attempts to adjust the rope, but not hitting the length, he tried to rectify his mistake, and was equally unsuccessful'.

Shocked by the hangman's conduct, many of the spectators cried out in detestation and for a while there was a serious danger that the 'untimely procrastination' would lead to a disturbance similar to that which had taken place at Johnston's execution sixteen years earlier.

'But, fortunately, at this critical period, Mr Brown, superintendent of public works, stepped forward, and with a firmness and presence of mind that does him the highest credit, pushed the executioner aside, and adjusted the rope to the

By courtesy of Edinburgh City Libraries

The hanging of William Burke, a notorious murderer, in Edinburgh in 1829 (from a contemporary print).

At the execution of Bartlett last Saturday, the hangman actually played the part of a buffoon to the populace, by sneeringly saying to the suspended corpse, 'Old chap, you are dead enough,' &c., and danced on the platform until the spectators actually repeatedly laughed - he patted him on his cheek, and heaved his cap from over his face, and shook hands with him, and gave him a box on the ear, which turned him round and round. Several women were on the platform to have their necks charmed by rubbing the dead man's hand over their wens as a cure; and it is a fact that children were acting the execution in the streets after it was over, by playing the part of Jack Ketch.

A report from a Gloucester newspaper, reprinted in *The Times* of 24 April 1837. The hangman's identity is not known.

scaffold with his own hand,' the *Courant's* report informs us.

The executioner then resumed his occupation, and placed the noose round the neck of the unfortunate culprit, who retained his wonted firmness during all this trying scene.

This lamentable course of bungling, however, had not terminated, for when the culprit jerked aside the fatal signal with which the drop should have given away almost simultaneously, a few moments dreadful suspense occurred, during which the miserable victim shook with a sort of convulsive tremor, at the same time stretching out his hands in the attitude of prayer, as if to snatch the last moment of intercession.

At last, however, the melancholy business terminated, and he died after one or two severe struggles.

Despite the bungling, there was no disorder on this occasion. Some small boys pelted the hangman with stones as he made his way from the scene, but he apparently suffered no serious injury. The scaffold was speedily removed and the street returned to normal.

Williams did not wait to be dismissed. On 28 July, it was reported to the Town Council that he had left the city with all his belongings, leaving the keys to his house in the Old Fishmarket Close with a neighbour. What became of him afterwards is unknown.

18. A Hangman Killed by an Alcoholic

John Williams was followed as hangman of Edinburgh by John Scott, who had formerly been hangman of Aberdeen. Scott's appointment is recorded in the Town Council Minutes for 28 July 1835: the date on which the Council was informed of his predecessor's departure. The entry gives details of his emoluments, but also states that he was to hold the post 'during the pleasure of the Council only'.

In addition to his free house in the Old Fishmarket Close, Scott was to receive wages of 12s a week from the town (the same as Simpson had been paid in 1816), together with fees of £1 1s for each execution and 10s 6d for each whipping. The minutes also inform us that he was to be paid 'the usual allowance' (£5 a year) by the Court of Exchequer for his services as dempster.

Scott was therefore several pounds a year better off as hangman of Edinburgh than he had been as hangman of Aberdeen. He was, however, considerably less well off than his brother functionary, Thomas Young, who had been receiving a salary of £50 a year since 1814. It is hard to see why this should have been so, but the Edinburgh magistrates obviously did not value their hangman as highly as the Glasgow authorities valued theirs.

A few days after being appointed to his new post, Scott had an execution to carry out. Elizabeth McNeill, who had been sentenced for poisoning, or attempting to poison, her husband, was hanged in Edinburgh on 3 August 1835. Fortunately, there was no bungling or mishap on this occasion, and Scott went on to hold the post for the next twelve years.

After the death of Thomas Young, Edinburgh became the only authority in Scotland to have a hangman among its officials, though Glasgow continued to pay a retainer to John Murdoch. The others just hired the services of either Scott or Murdoch (generally the latter) as the need arose, and so had only their fees and expenses to pay.

John Scott is known to have hanged William Perrie, a murderer, in Paisley in October 1837. This execution was attended by a large crowd of people, none of whom appear to have displayed any morbid excitement. A newspaper report describes their reaction to the hanging as follows:

> An involuntary shudder seemed to run through this immense crowd when the drop fell - all seemed shocked with the sight; and the general, if not the unanimous wish, seemed to be, that they might never have occasion to witness a similar scene.

Another execution carried out by Scott was that of a tinker named Wemyss, who was hanged in Edinburgh in 1840 for the murder of his wife. On this occasion, the execution was not performed at all satisfactorily.

'The rope being adjusted, and the cap drawn over (the condemned man's) face, after some hesitation he gave the signal,' says the *Caledonian Mercury's* report.

> An awful pause ensued - the executioner drew a bolt which turned out to be the wrong one. A groan of execration and hisses rose from the crowd. The executioner, evidently in desperation, tried by stamping with his heel to put the machinery of death in motion; but in vain.
> The commotion was increasing, when one of the officials in attendance ran up the steps of the scaffold, and withdrawing the bolt, an end was put to the agonies of the miserable man, and he was launched into eternity!

The incident undoubtedly led to a severe reprimand for Scott and he was almost certainly threatened with dismissal. Four years later, when James Bryce lay under sentence of death for the murder of his brother-in-law, the Edinburgh magistrates sent for Murdoch to carry out the execution. Scott must therefore have been unable to hang Bryce himself.*

It is quite likely that he was ill at the time, for he is known to have been in a poor state of health generally during his last years. He was nonetheless allowed to go on holding the post until his death, which took place on 12 August 1847.

John Scott did not die of natural causes. He was attacked and killed by an alcoholic named James Edey (spelt 'Edie' in the *Caledonian Mercury*), who lived in his own neighbourhood.

Edey, described as 'a broker and seller of watches', was a married man aged thirty-nine. After seven years of total abstinence, he had been induced by friends to drink some brandy on the night of 10 August, and was still drinking, or under the influence of drink, two days later.

'On Thursday his behaviour was of a most violent character,' says the *Mercury's* account of his attack on Scott.

> Notwithstanding the exertions of some of his neighbours he proceeded up the Cowgate in an excited manner, threatening and assailing all he met.
> His attention was unfortunately directed towards a man of the name of John Scott, who was standing at the bottom of the old Fishmarket Close, and who, it is presumed, was obnoxious to Edie from the odium which attached to his profession, as being the common executioner for the city.
> After a brief altercation (though it is also said that no words were exchanged),

---

* *The Life and Recollections of Calcraft the Hangman* (1880), p. 239, tells us that it was customary for Scott to be kept in jail for eight days prior to an execution, in order to ensure his attendance. If that is true, it obviously didn't have the desired effect in this case.

By courtesy of Edinburgh City Libraries

The hangman's house in Edinburgh, as depicted in an 1820 watercolour by James Skene.

Edie assaulted him in the most violent manner, knocking him down by repeated blows on the breast; and on Scott being carried to an adjoining shop, he was pursued thither by his assailant, who again struck him on the head, which produced immediate insensibility, and resulted in the death of Scott in a few minutes afterwards.

Edey was arrested and the following day made a statement in which he said he had no recollection of anything that had happened the day before. He admitted that he had known Scott, but denied bearing him any ill-will. He said he would never have struck him had he been in his senses.

On 24 August, the Town Council approved a payment to the hangman's widow of wages that would have been due to her husband for the previous two weeks had he still been alive. At the same time, it was agreed that she should be allowed to go on living in the house in the Old Fishmarket Close until the following Whit Sunday.

In November 1847, James Edey was tried at the High Court of Justiciary in Edinburgh for culpable homicide. The jury found him guilty, with a strong recommendation to leniency, and he was sentenced to nine months' imprisonment.

Nobody was appointed to fill the vacancy caused by Scott's death. There were, by this time, so few executions in Edinburgh that the city magistrates saw no further need to have a hangman of their own. Scott was thus the last member of his profession to hold an official post anywhere in Scotland.

19. A Hangman Aged Eighty-Four

John Murdoch was a Scottish hangman with no official post. He embarked upon his career about 1831, when he was already well into his sixties, and carried out his last execution some twenty years later. He was, as far as we know, the only British hangman to go on working until he was over eighty years of age.

Murdoch was a baker by trade. He arrived in Glasgow from the north of Scotland in the early 1830s, and, according to an obituary in the *Glasgow Herald*, worked in some lowly capacity for the City Corporation for a while. He is known to have carried out a hanging in Jedburgh in 1831, but it is unclear whether he was already living in Glasgow by this time.

For Murdoch, hanging could only have been a secondary occupation at first, as Scotland had so few executions and four Scottish towns still had hangmen of their own. At some stage during the early part of his career, however, the Glasgow magistrates began retaining him as a standby for Thomas Young, who had by now become unreliable.

When Young died, the magistrates decided that the city no longer needed a permanent hangman, but continued to pay Murdoch a monthly retainer of £1, with a fee of £10 for each person he hanged on their behalf. By this time, he and John Scott were the only practising hangmen left in the country and, as Scott's activities were largely confined to Edinburgh, provincial authorities turned increasingly to Murdoch when they needed the services of an executioner.

After living in Glasgow for a few years, Murdoch left the city and took up residence elsewhere. He is known to have lived in Paisley, Kilmarnock and Motherwell, among other places, during the course of his career, so he seems not to have stayed anywhere for long.

Murdoch enjoyed his work and was indifferent to the suffering of his victims. His *Herald* obituary tells us that news of a murder trial in Glasgow invariably drew him back to the city, in the hope that the accused would be convicted and sentenced to death. It also says that he was in the practice of lodging himself in prison, at the public expense, a week or ten days before an execution, so that the magistrates could feel sure that he would be available when he was needed.

Executions carried out by Murdoch include that of two murderers, Dennis Doolan and Patrick Redding, who were hanged on 14 May 1841, in a field outside Glasgow near the scene of their crime. Redding apparently died without a struggle, but Doolan's agony was protracted. Murdoch refused to accept that he was to blame for this.

'As Murdoch stood at the bottom of the scaffold immediately after the men had been thrown off, one of the authorities remarked that Doolan had not been properly handled, as he struggled and suffered much,' says the hangman's obituary.

> 'It's his ain fau't,' said Murdoch; 'nocht wad' ser' him but he wad tak' a jump when the drap gaed doon; but see, Sir, hoo kindly Redding's slippin' awa.'

In 1843, Allan Mair, aged eighty-two, was hanged in Stirling for the murder of his 'reputed wife', Mary Fletcher, aged eighty-five. Though Murdoch is known to have officiated in Stirling, he appears not to have done so on this occasion. A report in the *Stirling Journal* tells us that Mair's executioner wore a huge black mask: this suggests that he was not a regular hangman.

In April 1844, Murdoch hanged the murderer James Bryce in Edinburgh, as John Scott was unavailable or unfit to perform the duty himself. The execution took place at the usual site, at the head of Libberton's Wynd, before a crowd of 30,000 people.

Another execution carried out by Murdoch was that of John Wilson, a railway labourer, also convicted of murder, who suffered outside the County Jail in Jedburgh in October 1849. This was Jedburgh's first hanging for eighteen years, and a report in *The Times* mentions the fact that Murdoch - 'a feeble old man, and said to be upwards of 80 years old' - was the same hangman who had officiated on the previous occasion.

In Glasgow, at the end of January 1850, Murdoch hanged Margaret Lennox for the murder of her sister-in-law. In its report of that execution, the *Glasgow Herald* says of him:

> He is 82 years of age, and has a nerve like steel. Yesterday he had to mount the steps of the gallows by the help of a staff, but he did his duty with perfect coolness and composure.

In August the same year, Murdoch carried out another hanging in Edinburgh's Lawnmarket, John Scott being dead by this time. A report in *The Times* names him as the executioner, but says nothing about his age or infirmity. The condemned was William Bennison, who had been sentenced for the murder of his wife.

The last time that Murdoch officiated at an execution was in Glasgow in October 1851, when Archibald Hare was hanged for a murder committed in Blantyre. This particular execution is mentioned in Murdoch's *Herald* obituary, which tells us:

> He was then 84 years of age, and was so lame with rheumatism that he had to hirple after the criminal to the gallows by the aid of a staff; but once there, the old

fellow did his duty with nerves of steel.

An account of the proceedings in *The Times*, however, says that the culprit only died after a protracted struggle.

Besides Glasgow, Edinburgh, Stirling and Jedburgh, Murdoch is known to have hanged offenders in Inverness, Aberdeen, Ayr, Perth and Dundee. He also carried out executions at one time or another in various towns in the north of England, including Newcastle-upon-Tyne and Carlisle.

Following his retirement, he went to live in Bothwell in Lanarkshire. There he spent his last days, supported by monthly relief payments from the Glasgow Corporation. He died, aged eighty-nine, on 15 March 1856.

20. A Hangman for Forty-Five Years

William Calcraft was hangman of London and Middlesex from 1829 to 1874, making him Britain's longest-serving executioner on record. For the first fifteen months of his long tenure of office he held the post jointly with Thomas Cheshire, who had been appointed to succeed James Foxen less than two months earlier. Thereafter, he held the post on his own, without even the services of a regular assistant.

Calcraft was born in Little Baddow, a village near Chelmsford in Essex, on 10 October 1800. His parents were poor and had, in all, eleven children, only three of whom were still alive in 1850. William, the eldest, had little or no formal education, and although he learnt to read and write, his spelling and punctuation were always poor. At some stage, however, he learnt the trade of a shoemaker, which he was to follow, between executions, for much of his adult life.

Calcraft was married in Little Baddow in April 1824 and his wife Louisa, who was five years his senior, gave birth to their daughter Harriot just three months later. Within the next two years the couple moved to London, where they had a son, William, in 1826 and another son, James, in 1828.

We have no reliable information about how Calcraft made his living during his first years in London. Some accounts of his life say that he worked as a watchman at Reid's brewery in Clerkenwell; he is also said to have been a hawker of meat pies. Unfortunately, these accounts are quite untrustworthy and he may well have done neither of those things.

Calcraft's selection for the post of hangman took place during the week prior to 4 April 1829. He was one of two applicants considered by the Jails Committee of the Court of Aldermen, the other being an ex-soldier named Smith. Calcraft claimed that he had once carried out a double hanging in Lincoln and, according to a report in *The Observer*, 'the fact was properly authenticated'.

As Smith had no such experience, Calcraft was judged to be the more suitable candidate for the post. He was then aged twenty-eight and was described in a second report as 'a man of decent appearance'.

Though London now had two official hangmen, Calcraft appears to have carried out all or most of the London and Middlesex executions which took place in the next fifteen months, with Cheshire doing little or no work at all. Cheshire, in all likelihood, just acted as Calcraft's assistant from time to time until his death in July 1830.

At the beginning of Calcraft's career, the number of London and Middlesex prisoners who were hanged each year was, on average, about seventeen. After 1830, however, there were far fewer: just twelve in the three years 1831-3, none

Calcraft (selling pies) speaking to Foxen at a Newgate execution: a fictitious scene from the *Life and Recollections of Calcraft the Hangman* (1880).

In the early 1820s, England and Wales had over two hundred crimes which were punishable by death. By 1861, this number had been reduced to four: these were murder, treason, piracy with violence and setting fire to a dockyard or an arsenal. Since that time, there have been very few executions anywhere in Britain except for murder.

at all in 1834-6, three in 1837-9, four in 1840-2 and five in 1843-5. This fall in the number of executions was due to a progressive reduction, in the 1820s and 1830s, of the number of crimes punishable by death under English law.

Some whippings were still carried out by the hangman in the early part of Calcraft's career, but branding, mutilation and other punishments which he had previously inflicted were no longer used. Eventually, he lost the duty of whipping as well and his work thus became confined solely to hanging.

In return for his services to the Corporation of London, Calcraft was paid a guinea a week in wages (increased to £1 5s shortly before he retired), with a further guinea for each hanging and 2s 6d for each whipping; he is also believed to have had an allowance for whips and birch-rods while whipping remained one of his duties. At the same time, he received an annual retainer of £5 5s from the Surrey authorities, with an extra guinea for each hanging at Horsemonger Lane.

The first execution carried out by Calcraft at Newgate Prison was that of a murderess named Esther Hibner, which took place on 13 April 1829, just nine days after his appointment. Mrs Hibner, who had starved and flogged a young apprentice girl to death, behaved so violently after being sentenced that a straitjacket had to be used to restrain her. On the morning of her execution, she was carried to the gallows and hanged before a huge crowd. She apparently died almost immediately after the drop fell.

Another hanging at which Calcraft officiated early in his career was that of four men who suffered together, also at Newgate, on 31 December the same year. None of these offenders died quickly: in fact, they all struggled a great deal. One of the four was Thomas Maynard, the last person to be hanged for forgery in England.

The sharp decline in England's use of the death penalty naturally led to a reduction in Calcraft's income from the London and Surrey authorities. But England, like Scotland, now had very few hangmen left and Calcraft, being prepared to travel anywhere in the country, had far more offers of work from other towns than any previous holder of the post. And while his fee for a London or Surrey hanging was only £1 1s, he could get far more for hangings carried out elsewhere.

During the course of his long career, Calcraft is known to have hanged at least one person in each of the following towns: Aberdeen, Aldershot, Aylesbury, Beaumaris, Bedford, Bodmin, Brecon, Bristol, Bury St Edmunds, Cambridge, Cardiff, Carlisle, Castletown, Chatham, Chelmsford, Chester, Chipstead, Derby, Devizes, Dorchester, Dumfries, Durham, Edinburgh, Exeter, Glasgow, Glouces-ter, Greenlaw, Ipswich, Lancaster, Leicester, Lewes, Lincoln, Linlithgow, Liverpool, Maidstone, Manchester, Monmouth, Northampton, Norwich, Oxford, Perth, Reading, Salford, Shrewsbury, Swansea, Taunton, Winchester and Worces-ter.

Reports in *The Times*, from which this list has been largely compiled, show, too, that in some of these towns - Chelmsford, Exeter, Ipswich, Liverpool and Maidstone among them - Calcraft carried out executions on several different occasions.

Generally, for provincial, Welsh or Scottish hangings, he was paid at least £10 (sometimes it was as much as £21), together with his expenses. So, all in all, his income from hanging must have been quite considerable, in spite of the reforms of the 1820s and 1830s.

Notable criminals executed by Calcraft at Newgate include François Cour-voisier, a Swiss butler hanged in 1840 for the murder of his employer, Lord William Russell; Franz Müller, a German hanged in 1864 for Britain's first train murder, and Michael Barrett, a Fenian hanged in 1868 for his part in a bomb outrage at Clerkenwell Prison in which twelve people were killed and 120 injured. Barrett's was the last execution in Britain to be carried out in public.

Calcraft was also the executioner of Frederick and Marie Manning, who were hanged at Horsemonger Lane in 1849 for the murder of Marie's lover, and Dr Edward William Pritchard, who suffered in Glasgow in 1865 for poisoning his wife and mother-in-law. The execution of the Mannings was the subject of a famous letter of protest from Charles Dickens published in *The Times* the following day. Dickens later used Marie Manning as his model for Hortense, the murderous French maid in *Bleak House*.

The last hanging carried out at Execution Dock was apparently that of George James Davis and William Watts, who suffered for piracy on 16 December 1830. The use of the site as a place of execution was brought to an end by an Act of Parliament a few years later.

On 22 February 1864, at Newgate, Calcraft hanged five sailors (four Spaniards and a Turk), all of whom had been condemned for their involvement in a mutiny aboard the merchant ship *Flowery Land*, in the course of which the captain and five crew members were murdered. The hanging of the 'Five Pirates', as they were called, was the first execution of such a large number of people at Newgate for over forty years.

Calcraft usually gave his victims only a short drop and was thus responsible for many painful scenes of the sort which had occurred at the hanging of

EXECUTION. - Thursday morning the two unfortunate men, in pursuance of their sentence at the late Admiralty Sessions, underwent the last sentence of the law, viz. George James Davis, alias George Huntley; and William Watts, alias Charles Williams. In the early part of the morning they partook of a slight repast, and afterwards received the Sacrament. At half-past seven the Sheriffs arrived at Newgate. Davis, who was neatly dressed in a new blue suit, said he was going to suffer justly, and freely forgave every man. Watts was clad in a blue jacket, and white waistcoat and trowsers. He looked wan and remained silent, with the exception of expressing the united thanks of himself and companion for the kind treatment they had received. They were placed in the cart, and the cavalcade moved forward to the fatal spot. When they arrived upon the platform, they behaved with the greatest decorum till the bolt was withdrawn, and they were launched into eternity.

Bell's Life in London, 19 December 1830.

Maynard and his fellow sufferers. In evidence to the Royal Commission on Capital Punishment in 1864, it was stated that his method of hanging was much the same as if he had been hanging a dog.

The most shocking spectacle at which Calcraft officiated took place at Newgate on 31 March 1856, when he hanged a murderer named William Bousfield. Bousfield was very ill from an apparent suicide attempt (he had put his face into the fire in his cell) and was unable to walk unaided. Because of this, he was carried onto the scaffold on a chair, which was then placed under the fatal beam.

Unusually for him, Calcraft was nervous on this occasion, having received a threatening letter saying that he would be shot if he tried to perform his duty. With the condemned man still sitting on the chair, he hurriedly carried out his final preparations and released the drop without waiting for the usual signal. He then rushed back into the prison for his own safety.

But Bousfield was still alive and, despite his poor physical condition, he managed to draw himself up and get his feet onto the edge of the platform. He then tried desperately to raise his hands to the rope, but without success. A turnkey rushed over and pushed his feet back off, but Bousfield then raised himself the other side and gained a foothold there.

Calcraft was found and brought back to the scaffold; he then pushed the condemned man from the platform himself. Bousfield, however, did not give up his ghastly struggle for survival even then and succeeded in regaining his foothold at least once more. Finally, though, his legs were held down and his protracted ordeal was brought to an end.*

---

* Some accounts state that Bousfield got his feet back onto the platform four times; others that his legs were held down after the third time.

A pamphlet, published in 1863, with an illustration showing the procession to the gallows at Newgate.

No action was taken against Calcraft over this frightful incident. At a meeting of the Court of Aldermen the following day, one of the sheriffs expressed the view that 'no one was to blame, excepting it may be said that the nervous agitation and alarm under which the executioner acted led to the lamentable occurrence'. The Court apparently agreed with him.

Like Botting and Foxen, Calcraft collected his wages each week from Newgate Prison. Unlike them, however, he was not given his money over the prison gate, but was allowed to go inside the building to receive it: a sign that he was not held in such low esteem as they had been.

Calcraft lived for many years in Hoxton: in Devizes Street for some years prior to the mid-1850s and in Poole Street thereafter. He appears to have carried on his shoemaking trade from home.

In March 1850, while living at the first address, Calcraft was taken to court for neglecting and refusing to support his aged mother. Sarah Calcraft, who was in her seventies, was now an inmate of the Witham Union Workhouse in Hatfield Peverel, three miles south-west of Witham. The hearing, at Worship Street Police Court, began on 6 March.

Mr Shee, the Relieving Officer of the Union, told the court that Mrs Calcraft had only two sons, one of whom was William Calcraft: the other was an itinerant worker with no apparent means of affording her relief. The local Board of Guardians had therefore decided to proceed against the defendant for her maintenance, but he had refused to comply with its requisition. It had therefore become necessary for a summons to be taken out against him.

Mr Shee apparently had no difficulty convincing the magistrate, Mr Hammill, of the defendant's liability for his mother's support, but failed to produce evidence that Calcraft had the means to support her. Mr Hammill warned him that he would not feel justified in making an order against the defendant without such evidence and adjourned the case for a week to give the Relieving Officer an opportunity to produce it.

On 13 March, the day the hearing was to be resumed, the court was crowded with spectators. The Governor of Newgate was there to give evidence of Calcraft's income from the City; the hangman's mother was also there (which she had not been on the earlier occasion). The defendant, however, did not arrive on time and the Governor's evidence was given in his absence. The Governor told the court that Calcraft received a guinea a week from the Corporation of London for his 'public services', and that he (the witness) gave him his wages personally every Saturday.

By the time the Governor had finished giving his evidence, the defendant had still not appeared and Mr Hammill was about to issue a warrant for his arrest. But Calcraft suddenly walked into the courtroom and the hearing then continued.

'Sarah Calcraft, who was compelled by her infirmities to be seated during the

The hanging of Michael Barrett: the last execution in Britain to be carried out in public (from *The Illustrated Police News* of 30 May 1868).

examination, was then called, and stated, that she was 74 years of age, and had been for the last three weeks an inmate of the workhouse of Hatfield Peveril, in the Witham Union, having become totally destitute, and constrained in consequence to throw herself upon the parish,' says a report published in *The Times* the following day.

Previous to that she had been sheltered for two years by her married daughter at Hatfield, with whom, upon entering the workhouse, she had left the few trifling articles that had not already been sold to supply her immediate wants; and before that had addressed three letters to the defendant, whom she had not seen for about three years, requesting assistance, but she had not received anything from him, and he had not even answered one of her communications.

She had only one other child, a son, but he had been brought up to no regular employment, was sometimes in service, and generally jobbed about the country, earning a shilling in any manner he could.

The defendant, she believed, was in circumstances to support her, as, in addition to the salary he received from the corporation, he had another business, and carried on the trade of a boot and shoe maker.

After hearing this evidence, Mr Hammill asked the hangman whether he had any reasonable grounds for refusing to contribute to his mother's maintenance.

'Well, I should be very happy to support her if it was in my power, but it is not,' replied Calcraft. 'And as to what she says about the profits I derive from my shoemaking business, I can assure you that I have not earned a penny at that for a great number of weeks. I have sustained a very severe personal injury: in fact, you never saw such an arm as I have got. I can neither get my coat on nor off without assistance and, after being confined to my bed with it for more than two months, had a doctor's bill sent in to me for £10 3s 6d, which I am totally incapable of paying at present, and he must wait for it.

'I admit that I receive a guinea a week from the City, but that is all we have to live upon, and when you deduct out of that 4s 6d for rent, and the cost of a Sunday's dinner, you will find that there is not much left,' he continued. 'It is not from want of feeling that I don't support my mother. She was in much better circumstances than I am; she had a large quantity of good furniture and a number of silver spoons, and I can't see why she applied to the workhouse people at all.'

'Have you got any children to support?' asked the magistrate.

'Yes, I have got three of them,' said Calcraft.

'How old are they?'

'As old as you are.'

'Then, if that is the case, they cannot be much of a burden to you?'

'No, but they come sometimes, and, of course, put me to some expense extra.'

'Well, you are clearly liable for the support of your mother, which is rendered imperative by an Act as old as the reign of Elizabeth,' said Mr Hammill. 'And I feel it my duty to make an order upon you for the sum of 3s per week.'

'Ah, but you'll never get it from me! I can't pay it and, if you do, I must run in debt, I suppose.'

'I shall make an order upon you for the sum of 3s per week for your mother's support as long as she continues chargeable to the Union Workhouse, together with the costs attendant upon the present proceedings against you.'

'Oh, very well!' said the hangman. 'You may make your order if you like, but it's wholly out of my power.'

Mr Shee told the magistrate that the expenses which he had incurred in connection with the case totalled £1 9s 6d. Mr Hammill accepted this figure and agreed to its inclusion in his order. The hangman then turned to Mr Shee and said, 'Well, now, suppose I took my mother to keep myself, what would you allow me for her? Come, that's the point! Certainly, if you allow me something for her, I may be able to get on, perhaps.'

But Mr Shee said that he intended to adhere to the magistrate's order, as he believed Mrs Calcraft would prefer being in the union. And Mrs Calcraft agreed that that was so.

'Oh, dear, yes!' she said. 'I should not be alive a week in London, whereas I should be safe in the country if they even left me upon the common. I prefer being in the workhouse, for I am very comfortable there.'

The *Times* report tells us that, in spite of this snub, Calcraft then leant over his mother and expressed his willingness to take care of her, saying that he was very sorry she should have had to come to court at all. When the order had been made, an officer of the court tried to raise her from her chair, but the defendant pushed him aside and helped her from the court himself.

'There was,' the report concludes, 'a striking contrast between his compensating tenderness towards his mother and his rough coarseness to everybody else.'

Supported by her son, Sarah Calcraft remained in the workhouse until her death five years later. In view of his remarks about the condition of his arm, it is also worthy of note that a month after the resumed hearing Calcraft was able to carry out a double hanging in Cambridge.

Just a few months before these two court appearances, Dickens had referred to Calcraft disparagingly in a letter to *The Times*. This was not the letter published the day after the execution of the Mannings, but another one on the subject of capital punishment written a few days later. Mr Calcraft, the hangman, 'should be restrained in his unseemly briskness, in his jokes, his oaths, and his brandy', said the famous novelist. Presumably, Dickens had received reports of some misconduct on Calcraft's part which he thought was bad enough to justify such a stricture.

It must, however, be said that such behaviour was not characteristic of

Calcraft. Much that was written about him during his lifetime, and in the years following his death, suggests that he was, in general, fairly inoffensive. Some writers seem to have found him quite a likeable person.

'I can see him as I write, a mild, gentlefaced man, his eyes full and grey, though small and sweet in their expression,' wrote an anonymous clergyman in Dickens's own journal, *All the Year Round*, in 1868.

Arthur Griffiths, in *The Chronicles of Newgate* (1884), tells us that Calcraft was a kindly but simple-minded man who scarcely remembered what executions he had carried out. 'When he came to the prison for his wages his grandchildren often accompanied him, affectionately clinging to his hands,' says Griffiths. The same author also informs us that Calcraft was a keen angler and a devoted rabbit fancier and says that at one stage in his life he owned a pet pony which would follow him about like a dog.

A description of Calcraft in his early sixties is to be found in the *Carnarvon and Denbigh Herald* of 5 April 1862. This tells us that he was 'a man of middle height, rather broad-set', and then continues:

> His countenance is not at all repulsive, but has that fixedness of outline which is common to persons who perform deeds requiring great nerve. His hair is rather grey, and he wears his whiskers which are considerably whiter than the hair of his head, and rather long, all round his face. He would pass with a stranger for a respectable Englishman of ordinary moral stamp.

Calcraft sometimes professed to have qualms about his work. Following the execution of the Mannings, for example, as he left the prison, he was heard to say that he 'did not much like hanging a man and his wife'. On a later occasion, towards the end of his career, he claimed that he felt 'exceedingly pained' when called upon to carry out an execution. Whether he really did so, or just felt obliged to pretend he did, is not at all clear.

Calcraft's remarks on this second occasion were reported in the *Dundee Advertiser* of 29 April 1873. Calcraft had gone to Dundee to hang an offender named Thomas Scobbie, and was given quarters in the prison. But a few hours after his arrival, news was received that the condemned man's sentence had been respited.

The hangman remained at the jail for several more hours and during that time had conversations with a number of visitors. 'He entered very minutely into his experiences, stating that he felt exceedingly pained when called upon to perform the functions of his office,' says the *Advertiser's* report.

> It had, he said, afforded him much gratification to learn that the unfortunate prisoner whom he had come to hang had been respited.

Calcraft in old age: a photograph taken about 1870.

> It is only right, whilst mentioning the celebrities connected with the Old Bailey, that I should allude to one other personage. Rarely met with upon festive occasions, he was, nevertheless, accustomed to present himself after dinner on the last day of the sessions. He was a decently dressed, quiet-looking man. Upon his appearance he was presented with a glass of wine. This he drank to the health of his patrons, and expressed with becoming modesty his gratitude for past favours, and his hopes for favours to come. He was Mr. Calcraft, the hangman.
>
> From *Some Experiences of a Barrister's Life* (1882) by William Ballantine.

It is hard to believe that Calcraft was really gratified by this news. He had, after all, agreed to perform the execution when he was under no obligation to do so. It is, however, of interest to learn that he was willing to discuss his work so readily with people who were strangers to him, for his *Daily Telegraph* obituary states that he was 'of a taciturn disposition, particularly with respect to matters touching his profession'. Clearly, that was not the case.

Calcraft, by this time, was seventy-two years old and a very wellknown figure. When he arrived at Dundee West Railway Station later that day, to catch a train back to London, he found a large crowd waiting for him. According to the *Advertiser*, he was quite unperturbed by this:

> He inquired of one or two bystanders what the people wanted to see, and was told that he was the object of their solicitation. Evidently anxious that all should have the fullest opportunity of inspecting him, after taking his seat in a second-class carriage he rose to the window, and kept his head out till the train left the station. There was no display of feeling, and he had a compartment of the carriage all to himself.

Calcraft was not always given accommodation at prisons when he was away from home overnight on official business. On a visit to Taunton to carry out an execution there in 1867, he stayed at the County Inn, but left without paying his bill (13s 9d).

The landlord, a Mr Sulley, was determined to get his money, but Calcraft was equally determined not to pay him. Eventually, legal proceedings were started and the case was duly heard at the County Court in Taunton on 20 October 1869. This time Calcraft did not appear, but a letter in which he complained of being overcharged was read to the court. He was ordered to pay the full amount, the judge allowing him a month in which to do so.

Calcraft did not always carry out executions on his own, especially during the last years of his career. The person who usually assisted him at this time was Robert Ricketts Anderson, an eccentric Welshman who had changed his name from Evans and was known in his native Carmarthenshire as 'Evans the Hangman'.

Anderson had assisted Calcraft, at least occasionally, over a long period of time. He is also known to have carried out two triple executions on his own: the first in Gloucester in January 1874 (about four months before Calcraft's retirement), the second in Liverpool a year later.

The last time he assisted Calcraft was on 25 May 1874, when James Godwin, a hearth-rug maker, was hanged at Newgate for the murder of his wife. A letter from the Governor of Newgate to Anderson, held at the National Library of Wales, shows that it was Calcraft himself who had suggested that Anderson be employed on this occasion. It is dated 11 May and reads as follows:

It appears from the letter which Mr. Calcraft, the hangman, addressed to Mr. Sulley, of the County Inn, Taunton, respecting a bill incurred by him when staying in that town for the purpose of executing a criminal, that the office of hangman has not yet been placed under the regulations of the Civil Service Commissioners.

London, Sept. th28, 1869.

Sulley, i am quite a Shamed at your meanness of sending me that open peace of paper to expose me in that way to think that you want me to spend 2 or 3 pounds to com to your place to Pay you the sum of l4s. wich i never had half of it will Swear if i had you had half of it what did it coust me when whe ware out together you never spent one halfpenny and you to charge me that exorbant sum i suppose you thought of fritening me but i was born too near a wood to be fritened by an Owl the sum you charged me the Sheriff ought to have setteled long ago i have sent you the Beastley bit of paper you sent me in an invelope not open as you sent it me you can doo what you like with it as soon as it is convnant i will send you a post offic order for the over charge of 14s. with a check upon you for so mean an action. WS--WC. i never was served Such a mean action in all my life i never hat such a thing in my house before
                              mean   mean.

It will hardly be credited that, notwithstanding this exquisitely touching letter, it was decided at the county court at Taunton that Mr. Calcraft must pay the amount claimed by Mr. Sulley within a month. It was stated in court that Calcraft's trade had been slack lately. If so, we were not aware of it: there seem to be murders enough to support an army of hangmen. We suspect that if anybody is to blame, it is not the murderers, but the Home Secretary.

Pall Mall Gazette, 23 October 1869.

The Sheriffs are very desirous that Calcraft should have some assistance at an execution fixed for the 25th Inst. and Calcraft named you as the person he wished to be with him, and unless you hear to the contrary I shall expect to see you here on Saturday the 23rd Inst. by 10a.m.

Anderson was a man of private means who claimed to have personally devised some new technique of hanging which enabled Calcraft - under Anderson's own direction - to perform his duties more humanely than he would otherwise have done. The claim was made in a letter to the Home Secretary of the day, published, at the writer's own request, in *The Times* of 21 December 1875:

For upwards of 20 years I have, from humane motives, devoted my attention to executions, and have attended nearly all the principal ones that have taken place in this kingdom during that long period, giving my advice and assistance to the executioner, and in no single instance where I have been present has the slightest failure occurred or any unnecessary suffering been caused the unfortunate culprit. In cases where I have occasionally acted alone - in triple executions, for instance, as at Liverpool, Glocester, &c., - my plans have been completely successful.

Robert Ricketts Anderson (on right): a photograph reproduced by kind permission of Robert Evans of Llanstephan, Carmarthenshire, a great-grandson of the hangman.

What his 'plans' were, Anderson didn't say, but he went on to claim that they had been adopted in a number of prisons and found to be effective. He then went back to the subject of himself and his experiences, claiming to have made personal sacrifices for the sake of the condemned:

> My career has attracted the notice of the Press, by which I have been styled 'the Amateur,' 'the Doctor,' 'the Medical Executioner,' and other *aliases*, by writers who assumed to know my personal history. The fact is, I was intended for the medical profession, but did not adopt it, as I have private means. The taking part in this business has not been from a mercenary, but from a humane motive; and it has cost me a large amount of time and money, and has been a source of annoyance to some of my best friends. I, however, have persevered in what I felt to be a humane course, and my efforts were appreciated by one, at least, eminent prison philanthropist, the late Mr. Wright, whose portrait, in his acts of mercy, now adorns the Council Chamber of the Guildhall.

Anderson had begun his letter by deploring the employment of 'ignorant, brutish persons' as hangmen, though without giving any indication of who he had in mind. He ended it by proposing that executions should be carried out by prison officers, saying that he personally would then be willing to give the benefit of his experience, assistance and advice wherever it was required. The offer failed to bring about the change that he was advocating.

Anderson was the son of a Carmarthen solicitor. Born about 1816, he was better educated than most other hangmen, but had abandoned his studies in favour of a life of leisure and sensation-seeking. He had been married twice and boasted of many sexual conquests. He was also an enthusiastic supporter of prize-fighting.

There is no evidence to support Anderson's claim that Calcraft hanged people more humanely under his influence. We know from eyewitness reports - for journalists were sometimes allowed to watch executions at this time - that several of Calcraft's later victims suffered acutely. These include James Godwin, who took several minutes to die: during that time, his body was convulsed and he tried repeatedly to raise his hands to his throat.

We also know that one of Anderson's triple hangings was not as successful as he claimed. This was the one in Gloucester, which took place on 12 January 1874. 'The woman lived some time longer than the others, doubtless owing to her spare figure,' says a report in *The Times*.

Shortly after Godwin's execution, Calcraft resigned from his official post and was granted a pension of 25s a week by the City Corporation. He was then seventy-three years of age and had been a widower for four years; his wages had been raised from 21s to 25s a week just three months earlier. He never hanged anyone else.

In all, Calcraft must have officiated at well over 300 executions during the course of his career. Richard A. Jeffery, a descendant of his, has identified 268 cases in which he was named as the hangman, but says in a *Family Tree Magazine* article, published in September 1995, that he believes the true total to be much higher. All but the last thirty-six of these executions were carried out in public.

Calcraft was the last hangman to receive weekly wages from the Corporation of London. His successor, William Marwood, was, however, paid an annual retainer of £20 by the City, in addition to his fee of £10 for each execution. Marwood, a native of Horncastle, in Lincolnshire, was a pioneer of the long-drop method of hanging, which was soon to come into general use in Britain.

Calcraft died on 13 December 1879, at his home in Poole Street, Hoxton, where he had lived for over twenty years. He was seventy-nine years old. His daughter and two sons survived him.

The old executioner was the subject of a full-length work, *The Life and Recollections of Calcraft the Hangman*, issued in thirty parts from the office of

William Marwood (from *The Life and Career of Marwood the Exec-utioner*, 1883).

the *Illustrated Police News* after his death. This, unfortunately, contains much obvious fiction, and so is of little use as a source of information. A number of pamphlets published over the course of his career, purporting to give details of his life, are unreliable for the same reason.

Robert Ricketts Anderson carried out no more hangings after the triple execution in Liverpool, mentioned in his letter to the Home Secretary. In fact, he seems to have taken no active part in executions at all after that, though he continued to take a keen interest in them for the rest of his life. He died at the age of eighty-five on 26 August 1901.

21. The Last York Hangmen

Nathaniel Howard, who succeeded Coates as hangman of York, was a coal porter aged about sixty at the time of his appointment. The first execution he carried out was that of James Bardsley, or Bradsley, aged twenty-eight, who was hanged at the Castle on 11 April 1840 for the murder of his father.

Howard, a resident of the city, had been appointed hangman in haste while Bardsley was already under sentence of death. He carried out his execution wearing prison dress, probably in keeping with local custom, as the York hangman was traditionally a pardoned capital offender. The *York Courant's* report of the proceedings says that he 'appeared much affected both before and after the performance of his task'.

Clearly, he found the experience disagreeable, but he continued as hangman in spite of it and remained in the post for the next thirteen years. In that time, eleven more executions took place in York, including a triple one on 7 August 1841 and a double one on 9 April the following year. Howard is also known to have officiated at a hanging in Newcastle-upon-Tyne in August 1850, and may well have carried out others elsewhere.

The last execution he performed was that of Henry Dobson, aged twenty-seven, who had been condemned for the murder of a teenage girl in Wakefield. Dobson was hanged on 9 April 1853, the hangman carrying out his duties 'somewhat tardily' (so says William Knipe, in his *Criminal Chronology of York Castle,* 1867). When the drop fell and the rope tightened round his neck, the condemned man struggled violently.

The spectacle was, in fact, so shocking that Howard was afterwards removed from his post. The *York Herald* of 16 April, reporting the hangman's dismissal, stated: 'The painful exhibition of last Saturday, when Dobson was executed, showed that, from old age and infirmity, he was totally incapable to perform the duties of his "responsible situation."' Howard, who was now seventy-three years of age, died just six days later, on 22 April.

York had only one more hangman of its own after Howard: that was Thomas Askern, who was not appointed until August 1856. The city had had no executions in the meantime and there may well have been doubts about whether it really needed such a functionary. Eventually, though, there *was* a hanging to be carried out and the vacant post was then filled.

Askern was not, as some publications suggest, a convicted criminal: he was actually in prison for debt prior to his appointment as hangman. It is not known how long he remained a prisoner after his appointment, but it is clear from newspaper reports that he was free and living in Maltby, near Rotherham, by

January 1859. His release may well have been obtained for him in return for his acceptance of the post.

The offender under sentence of death at the time of Askern's appointment was William Dove, a notorious wife-killer. Dove was hanged at York Castle on 9 August 1856, before a crowd of between fifteen and twenty thousand people. The new hangman carried out his duty satisfactorily, the condemned man hardly suffering at all after the drop had fallen.

Askern went on to hold the post for over twenty years, and so, like Calcraft, officiated at both public and private hangings. But executions in York were even more infrequent in his time than they had been in Howard's, and although Askern is known to have carried out some in other towns - including at least four in Durham - his total was probably not much over twenty.

Several of these were performed less competently than Dove's, with the condemned suffering the same slow death as Dobson. In the case of John Hannah, who was hanged just four months after Dove, there were (says Knipe) 'some protracted struggles'; when Joseph Shepherd was hanged on 3 April 1858, there was 'a considerable amount of struggling'. Such incidents, in fact, continued to occur throughout Askern's career, showing that his technique was no better than Calcraft's.

In June 1864, in Edinburgh's Lawnmarket, Askern hanged George Bryce, who had been convicted of murdering a woman in Ratho, Midlothian. It was Edinburgh's first execution for over ten years. 'The drop was one of unusual length, and the scaffold being screened up to a certain height, the body was withdrawn from public view immediately on the bolt being drawn,' says a report in *The Times*.

> A thrill of horror went through the crowd at the fatal plunge, and some groans were uttered for the executioner, who showed the greatest coolness.

Somehow, *The Times* was able to ascertain that on this occasion the prisoner died after just a few slight struggles.

In September of the same year, Askern carried out a double hanging at Armley Jail, in Leeds. This particular execution was attended by an enormous number of people, many of whom had travelled from other towns in order to be present. In this case, too, there was a screen to prevent the condemned from being seen by the crowd after the drop had fallen.

'The gallows was enveloped in black cloth,' *The Times* of 12 September informs us.

> A screen which surrounded the floor of it hid the lower half of the men's bodies completely, and when the bolt had been drawn they fell out of sight entirely.

In spite of this, however, the reporter was able to say that one of the culprits 'appeared to die almost instantaneously', while the other struggled for two or three minutes.

In March 1865, when Askern hanged Matthew Atkinson, another wife-killer, in Durham, the rope broke and the prisoner fell fifteen feet to the ground. He apparently suffered no injury as a result of this, and after a delay of twenty minutes the drop was raised so that he could be hanged again.

Shortly afterwards, Askern reappeared on the scaffold and attached a new rope to the fatal beam. Then the condemned man ascended the scaffold for the second time and placed himself in position without assistance. This time the rope held and Atkinson died in less than a minute.

The worst incident of Askern's career occurred at his last execution of all. This was at Armley Jail on 3 April 1877, when he hanged John Henry Johnson, a thirty-seven-year-old fent dealer who had shot and killed an acquaintance in Bradford. The hanging was attended by six reporters who had been allowed into the prison to watch the proceedings.

As in Atkinson's case, the rope broke at the first attempt and the condemned man fell to the ground. The chaplain immediately called upon the small group of spectators to pray for him, then disappeared behind the black cloth which concealed him from their view.

'Johnson was heard groaning, and the governor directed a chair to be brought,' *The Times* reported the following day.

> While the chaplain was praying that faith and fortitude might be granted to the poor wretch during this horrible interval, search was made for another and a surer rope. After a lapse of about 10 minutes a new and thicker rope was fastened to the cross beam, and Johnson was led from beneath the drop. With wonderful firmness he re-ascended the 14 steps of the scaffold. The white cap yet obscured his face, but it did not prevent his voice being audible in prayer. The fresh noose was soon adjusted about his neck, and the fatal bolt again withdrawn.

Unlike Atkinson, however, Johnson did not die quickly at the second attempt. It was not until five minutes had elapsed that the convulsive movements of his body finally ended.

Despite this terrible performance, Askern seems to have been allowed to stay on in his post until his own death over eighteen months later. But Yorkshire had only one execution during that time - that was at York Castle in April 1878 - and it was not Askern, but William Marwood, who officiated on that occasion.

Marwood, by this time, was far more experienced than any other practising hangman in Britain, having already carried out executions all over the country. He nonetheless bungled this one, with the result that the condemned, Vincent

Knowles Walker, suffered for several minutes as he died of strangulation.

Askern himself died in Maltby, at the age of sixty-two, on 6 December the same year. He was, apparently, the last hangman to hold a provincial post anywhere in Britain.

22. Smith of Dudley

George Smith was another of Calcraft's contemporaries. A Black Country hang-man for over thirty years, he was sometimes called 'Smith of Dudley' and sometimes 'Throttler Smith'. His most celebrated victim was Dr William Palmer, the notorious 'Rugeley Poisoner' hanged at Stafford Jail in 1856.

Born in 1805, Smith was actually a native of Rowley Regis, two miles to the south-east of Dudley, and lived for most of his life in the village of Oakham, on the outskirts of that town. In his youth, he worked for a local shoemaker for a while, but on his death certificate he is described as an agricultural labourer. He is also known to have practised as a cow-doctor for many years.

He was, however, a dissolute man, who frequented low taverns and kept bad company. His parents, who were respectable people (or so it is claimed), had disowned him while he was still a young teenager and continued to regard him as a black sheep for the rest of their lives.

Smith apparently carried out his first execution (a double one) at Stafford Jail on 11 April 1840, while he was himself a prisoner there for failing to maintain his wife and child. The two culprits, James Owen and George Thomas, had been convicted of a brutal murder committed aboard a canal boat, as had a third man whose sentence was commuted.

Smith's name does not appear in newspaper reports of this execution, nor does it seem to have been published at all until after Palmer's death sixteen years later - and even then it was given incorrectly as *John* Smith. The case of Owen and Thomas is nonetheless referred to in a report of Smith's own death, in 1874, as the one in which he made his first appearance as hangman.

A year after the execution of Owen and Thomas, Smith carried out another hanging in Stafford: that of Matthew Fowles, aged twenty-two, who had been convicted of the murder of his landlady. After that, though he had no official post, he was accepted as Staffordshire's regular hangman, and remained so for the next thirty-two years.

During the course of his career, Smith also officiated at hangings in other counties, generally in the Midlands, but occasionally further afield. The earliest known hanging carried out by him outside Staffordshire was in April 1841, when he hanged Bartholomew Murray, a youth of eighteen, in Chester. He is described in a report of that execution as 'a tall, stout man, dressed in white barragon', and is said to have been 'a practitioner from Staffordshire, and the same who carried the law into effect upon Fowles'.

Despite the length of his career, Smith didn't hang anywhere near as many people as Calcraft. His total is sometimes given as just under sixty, but the true figure may have been even lower than that. In Staffordshire, at any rate, he hanged only nine people between April 1840 and April 1845, and eleven during the twenty-eight years that followed. All of these executions, with the exception of the last, took place at the front of Stafford Jail: the last was carried out privately, inside the prison, in 1872.

One notable offender hanged by Smith in Stafford was thirty-six-year-old Charles Moore, who suffered for his part in the murder of an elderly couple who had befriended him. Moore's execution took place on 9 April 1853, and was attended by many people from other parts of the county.

'On Friday night a considerable number of persons arrived in Stafford, and lodgings near the gaol, especially in houses commanding a view of the place of execution, were in high request,' says a report in the *Staffordshire Advertiser.*

> During all the hours of the night stragglers on foot and parties in every description of conveyance, incessantly poured in. About four o'clock on Saturday morning the more anxious of the spectators began to take up positions near the barricades erected across all the approaches to the prison about 20 yards from the principal entrance, in the front of which the 'drop' was erected.
>
> From that hour up to the time fixed for the execution - 8 o'clock - a continuous stream of spectators flowed from all quarters towards the gaol. The early trains from the north and south of the county also brought large numbers: though the 'special train' from the south, which was heavily laden, arrived about a quarter of an hour after the execution, greatly to the disappointment of hundreds who had come expressly for the purpose of seeing it.

There were nonetheless about 10,000 people present when the drop fell. The condemned man struggled convulsively for a few moments before he died.

Palmer's execution, three years later, attracted far more spectators than Moore's: two or three times as many, in fact. Palmer was a thirty-two-year-old physician and a habitual gambler: he had been convicted of murdering a fellow racegoer for his winnings, but is believed to have killed up to thirteen other people as well. The crowd greeted him with hostile shouts, but Palmer was unmoved by them. Before being turned off, he shook hands with the hangman, saying, 'God bless you!'; and then, when the bolt was drawn, he died without a struggle.

The *Advertiser's* report of that hanging tells us: 'The man who officiated as executioner on this occasion has performed the office several times at Stafford, and hung Moore for the Ash Flatts murder. He is a large man, in advanced middle age, and wore a long white smockfrock.' A report in *The Times* describes the hangman as 'a tall, broad-shouldered, elderly man, with short gray hair'; it also mentions his white smockfrock and says that he was a labouring man living in Dudley.

The hanging of William Palmer (from *Mysteries of Police and Crime*, 1898, by Arthur Griffiths).

Another Stafford execution carried out by Smith was that of George Jackson, a former soldier aged twenty, who had killed and robbed a man near the village of Abbots Bromley. Jackson was hanged in August 1857.

During the night preceding the execution, there was heavy rain in Stafford. But the gallows was erected outside the jail just the same, and vehicles kept arriving in the town from all directions. Smith and a companion spent part of the night at The Greyhound Inn, where their behaviour was such that the police were called to eject them. Four policemen were involved in the incident.

A crowd started to gather at the place of execution at an early hour, and, although the rain continued to fall heavily, there were four or five thousand people there by the time the hanging was due to take place.

Jackson put up a violent struggle, sobbing and groaning, and was carried the last few yards to the gallows with his feet tied. A chair had by this time been brought onto the drop and he was forced down onto it and held there while Smith set about his final preparations. But the culprit went on fighting desperately and at one point managed to remove the cap from his face. After it had been replaced, his hands were held down until the drop fell.

In Warwick, in August 1860, Smith hanged a man named Francis Price, who had committed a murder in Birmingham. The culprit died almost instantaneously, but the drop had been released unexpectedly while he was praying. This shocked many of the spectators and Smith was afterwards attacked at the local railway station.

'It appears that the executioner, Smith, after receiving his fee, proceeded to the Great Western Railway Station, to return to West Bromwich, and that he was recognised by some of the people waiting for the cheap train to Birmingham, due at 1.17 p.m.,' the *Warwick and Warwickshire Advertiser* of 25 August reported.

> He had a bundle of clothes in his hand which were supposed to be those which Price wished to be given to the mother of the murdered girl, but which proved to be a suit of his own. He stood on the edge of the platform, and a strong fellow mounted the balustrade, jumped upon him, and bore him down on to the line, to which some twenty or thirty other men soon made their way.
>
> The 12.50 goods train, which does not stop at Warwick, had not arrived, and one or two other trains were also due. Some of the ring-leaders threatened to push the executioner under the engine when it came up, whilst others vowed vengeance upon him for drawing the bolt before Price had time to finish his prayer, and one or two accused him of pulling the culprit's legs.*

The Station Master, a Mr Chilton, managed to rescue Smith from his assailants

---

* The crowd could see only the head and shoulders of the condemned man after the drop had fallen.

and locked him in the second-class waiting-room. But the disturbance outside continued until Mr Chilton put Smith on a train to Leamington, to prevent him from falling back into the hands of the mob.

In January 1866, Smith acted as Calcraft's assistant at the hanging of a man named Southey in Maidstone. It was snowing in the town that day, and a bitter wind was blowing. Because of this, the execution attracted only five hundred people.

In August of the same year, in Stafford, Smith hanged William Collier, a young poacher who had shot and killed a local landowner. It was the third execution to take place in Stafford that year, and the sixth since Jackson's in 1857. Unfortunately, there was a mishap, the rope slipping from the beam at the first attempt, so that the condemned man fell to the ground under the platform. The accident caused much dismay among the officials in attendance and indignation among the spectators.

Collier apparently landed on his feet, for when Smith went down to him after just a moment's hesitation, he found him leaning against the boards of the scaffold. The hangman quickly removed the rope from his neck and the white cap from his face, while the chaplain, who had followed him down from the platform, resumed his ministrations.

A warder took the rope and, with the aid of a ladder, fastened it to the beam of the gallows so that the culprit could be hanged again. Collier was then brought back up onto the platform and Smith set about his final preparations for the second time.

Despite loud protests from the crowd, it was not long before the drop fell again, and this time there was no mishap. One account of the proceedings says that about four and a half minutes elapsed between the first fall and the second; another says that it was six minutes. However long it was, the condemned man appeared to be unaware of what had happened to him. His whole attention, according to *The Times*, 'seemed to be absorbed in replying to the prayers repeated by the priest'.

In 1868, Smith assisted Calcraft at Britain's first two private executions: the first in Maidstone on 13 August, the second at Newgate on 8 September. He then took no part in any more executions for nearly four years.

On 13 August 1872, in Stafford, he hanged Christopher Edwards, a locksmith aged thirty-five, who had battered his wife to death in a fit of jealousy. A report of that execution states that the gallows - 'a hideous-looking structure' - was erected at the north end of the jail and that the culprit 'struggled much longer than is usually the case'. This was Stafford's first hanging since Collier's and the last to be carried out there by Smith.

The following day, Smith assisted Calcraft for the last time: again in Maidstone, but this time at a triple execution. On that occasion, two of the condemned

George Smith: a painting from an original photograph.

died instantly, but the third struggled for over ten minutes.

Thereafter, Smith carried out only five more hangings: two in England and three in Ireland. The first was in Warwick, where he executed Edward Hancock, another wife-murderer, in January 1873; the second was in Aylesbury, Buckinghamshire, where he hanged Henry Evans, also for wife-murder, on 4 August the same year. The other three all took place later in August 1873, two of them in what is now the Irish Republic, the third in Northern Ireland.

At Hancock's execution, a drop of less than three feet was given, and the condemned man, according to a local newspaper, was 'long in dying'. In one of the Irish cases, the rope was too long and had to be pulled up after the drop had fallen, as the culprit's feet were touching the floor under the scaffold.

'Smith of Dudley' died at his home in Oakham on 3 April 1874. A report of his death appeared in the *Derby and Derbyshire Gazette* of 10 April, referring to him as 'George Smith, "cow-leech," and the executioner of Palmer': it said he was seventy years of age and that he had retained his faculties until a day before his death. His death certificate, however, gives his age as sixty-nine and his occupation as 'agricultural labourer'.

Smith was a wellknown character locally and lives on in legend in the Dudley area.

Conclusion

Calcraft, Askern and Smith were the last British hangmen to carry out executions in public. It is therefore appropriate that this study should end with them.

Of the hangmen of more recent times, much is already known. In general, they were far more skilled than their oldtime predecessors, and carried out their duties speedily and humanely. A number of them attracted a lot of public interest as individuals, and several wrote their memoirs, either for book publication or in the form of newspaper serials. It has nonetheless been contended by some writers on the subject that they were still disesteemed figures, like those of the more distant past.

'The Executioner is a person whom no man loves and whom all men shun,' says an article published in the *Law Journal* in 1926.

> Even those members of the community who maintain most relentlessly the necessity of retaining capital punishment in the interests of the public security nevertheless do not show in practice any greater relish for the society of the hangman than do their fellows. Every soldier dislikes being selected for a shooting party. It is difficult to conceive of any woman being courted by and consenting to marry one who had already assumed this ghastly office. And if a hangman had children one feels reasonably certain they would keep in the dark the vocation of their parent.

Brian Bailey, in a sneering work entitled *Hangmen of England* (W. H. Allen, 1989) - not to be confused with Horace Bleackley's *un*sneering book of the same title - refers to our modern executioners collectively as 'ritual manslayers' and claims that they were 'naturally shunned by the public at large, even when the public in its ignorance supported the death penalty'.

The *Law Journal* article even gives details of a civil action in which the court allegedly accepted that the hangman was a figure of low standing:

> A respectable citizen had alighted at an inn in the City of Norwich the night before an execution. One of the bystanders, noticing a real or fancied resemblance to the executioner of the day, said loudly: 'You are Jack Ketch.' The citizen protested that he was not Jack Ketch, but the defamer persisted in saying that he was, and a mob who quickly collected proceeded to duck in the horsepond this unfortunate victim of mistaken identity.
>
> Their victim sued his traducer for damages for slander; there was no doubt of the special damage; but the defence pleaded by way of demurrer that the allegation could not possibly be defamatory. 'The Executioner,' they alleged, 'is a public official, necessary to the security of the State, and it is no more a libel to describe

a man as an executioner than to say that he is a judge.'

But the Court rejected this contention. They held that the charge of being a hangman was calculated to bring its victim into 'hatred, ridicule and contempt,' and therefore - if not in fact justified as true - was undoubtedly actionable as defamation, whether libel or slander depending on the medium of the accusation.

The author doesn't tell us when this case is supposed to have occurred (the phrase 'the executioner of the day' suggests that it was some time prior to 1926); nor does he give the source of his information. We therefore can't check to see if the story is true.

It is, however, undeniable that even our modern hangmen were shunned in *some* quarters. James Berry of Bradford, whose career lasted for eight years (1884-92), is known to have had to move home more than once because his neighbours were hostile towards him. John Ellis of Rochdale, the executioner of Dr Crippen, found that at social gatherings people stared at him and avoided shaking his hand. From the social point of view, being a hangman was 'a bad business', he concluded.

Even so, from Calcraft onwards, our hangmen do not seem to have had difficulty finding other work when they wanted it. Calcraft himself worked as a shoemaker between executions, Marwood as a cobbler, Ellis as a hairdresser. The late Albert Pierrepoint, who hanged over four hundred people before retiring in 1956, kept a public-house in Oldham called Help The Poor Struggler. Berry, after leaving the profession, gave public lectures on hanging.

Marwood actually exploited his reputation as a hangman in order to attract more customers to his shop. Outside the shop he displayed a sign which said *Crown Office*; inside he exhibited several of his used ropes. Some people, no doubt, objected to this, but Marwood obviously felt that it brought him more customers than it repelled.

Nor was it necessarily true that a hangman's children would be ashamed of their father's vocation, as the *Law Journal* article suggests. Albert Pierrepoint, born near Bradford in 1905, *was* the son of a hangman and was not at all ashamed of the fact.

Pierrepoint tells us in his memoirs, *Executioner: Pierrepoint* (George G. Harrap & Co., 1974), that during his summer holidays when he was eleven (he was then living in Huddersfield) he began reading his father's reminiscences in *Thomson's Weekly News*. On returning to school at the end of the holidays, he says, he wondered whether he would be treated differently from usual as a result of being 'the son of a celebrity'. As it happened, he was *not* treated differently, either by his classmates or by the masters.

Not long afterwards, his class was set an essay to write, entitled 'What I should like to do when I leave school'.

'I gazed pretty blankly at the paper,' he tells us. 'The rest of the class seemed all set, heads bent down industriously as they got on with their compositions. I dipped my pen. "When I leave school I should like to be the Official Executioner..." I found myself writing.'

The anecdote ends as follows:

> Mr. Hardcastle, the schoolmaster, a short, spectacled man, was roaming round the classroom. He stopped behind me and read my essay over my shoulder. He smiled and continued to walk round the class. Towards the end of the period he came back and read some more. I had always thought he was a stern man, but he patted me gently on the back and walked away, still with a quiet smile on his face. I handed in the essay, and realised that I had actually committed an ambition to paper.

It is clear from all this that our modern hangmen were nowhere near as widely shunned as some people like to think. In most cases, they were probably no more despised than policemen or prison officers.

The last hangings in Britain took place in 1964 and our last surviving former hangman, Syd Dernley, died thirty years later. Dernley was a native of Mansfield Woodhouse, Nottinghamshire. Born in 1920, he worked as a welder in a colliery for thirty years, then ran a post office in Mansfield until his retirement at the age of sixty.

Dernley's career as a hangman lasted for only four years (1949-53) and during that time he acted only as an assistant executioner. He nonetheless tells us in his memoirs, *The Hangman's Tale* (Robert Hale Ltd, 1989):

> Even after all these years I am still pointed out to people and I have a little chuckle to myself when I find somebody in a pub staring at me in that familiar way and I wonder who has been talking to them.

He then goes on to say this about other people's attitudes towards him:

> Public reaction has always been overwhelmingly favourable; for every person who backs away from me, there are half a dozen who wish to shake me by the hand and buy me a pint. Most people tell me they think I did a good job and it should be brought back. Some no doubt say, 'Cruel sod' when I have turned my back, but that does not bother me.

At the time his memoirs were published, Dernley was the treasurer of his local Conservative Club.

Sources of Information

1. EARLY HANGMEN

Pegge, Samuel: *Curialia Miscellanea* (1818), pp. 331-48.

Madox, Thomas: *The History and Antiquities of the Exchequer* (2nd ed., 1769), pp. 372-5.

Calendar of the Patent Rolls, Henry VI, IV, 426.

Marks, Alfred: *Tyburn Tree: Its History and Annals* (1908), pp. 6-26.

Bateson, Mary (editor): *Borough Customs* (1904-6), I, 73-6.

Blount, Thomas: *Fragmenta Antiquitatis* (1784 ed.), pp. 272-3.

Miscellanea Genealogica et Heraldica, 1874, pp. 203-4.

Andrews, William: *Old-Time Punishments* (1890), pp. 231-45.

Wriothesley, Charles: *A Chronicle of England* (edited by William Douglas Hamilton) (1875-7), I, 84-5.

Hall, Edward: *Hall's Chronicle* (1809 ed.), p. 826.

Stow, John: *The Annales of England* (1592 ed.), p. 972.

Dictionary of National Biography (refs. *Anne Boleyn* and *Margaret Pole*).

Grose, Francis and Astle, Thomas (editors): *Antiquarian Repertory* (1809), IV, 501-20.

Machyn, Henry: *The Diary of H. Machyn* (1848), p. 109.

Bleackley, Horace: *The Hangmen of England* (1929), p. 3.

Fraser, Antonia: *Mary Queen of Scots* (Panther ed., 1970), pp. 623-4.

Chester City Record Office, ref. *ML/1/99*.

The Gentleman's Magazine, 1731, p. 178.

The York Courant, 27 March and 10 April 1739.

Calendar of Common Council Book, Newcastle, 1699-1718 (Tyne and Wear County Archives Dept., ref. *589/6*).

Sykes, John and Fordyce, T.: *Local Records* (1866-76), I, 129.

Cameron, Joy: *Prisons and Punishment in Scotland* (Canongate Publishing Ltd., 1983), pp. 1-42.

Fleming, J. S.: *Old Nooks of Stirling* (1898), pp. 39-54.

Marwick, J. D. (editor): *Extracts from the Records of the Burgh of Glasgow, 1573-1642* (1876), pp. 233-4.

2. FATHER AND SON

Notes and Queries, 2nd Series, XI, 445-8.

Partridge, Eric: *A Dictionary of Historical Slang* (Penguin ed., 1972) (ref. *derrick*).

Brewer's Dictionary of Phrase and Fable (Cassell ed., 1952) (ref. *Derrick*).

Jeaffreson, John Cordy (editor): *Middlesex County Records* (1886-92), II, xvii-xviii, xx-xxi; III, xvii-xviii, xx-xxii.

O'Donoghue, E. G.: *Bridewell Hospital* (1929), p. 11 and Notes.

Middlesex County Records: Calendar of Sessions Rolls, Sessions Registers and Gaol Delivery Registers (typewritten series, Guildhall Library), Sections 495 to 500, for December 1610 to April 1611, pp. 68, 82, 118; Sections 505A to 507, for the year 1611, p. 54.

Le Hardy, William (editor): *Calendar to the Sessions Records (County of Middlesex)* (1935-41), II, 279, 305; III, 104-5, 329.

Calendar of State Papers (Domestic Series), 1611-18, p. 428.

Dictionary of National Biography (ref. *Richard Brandon*).

Thomason Tracts (British Library), *E.561. (12)* and *(14).*

Sidney, Philip: *The Headsman of Whitehall* (1905).

Muddiman, J. G. (editor): *Trial of King Charles the First* (1928), pp. 147-8, 167-83.

Ellis, Sir Henry (editor): *The Obituary of Richard Smyth* (1849), p. 35.

3. THE ORIGINAL JACK KETCH

Notes and Queries, 2nd Series, XI, 445-8.

Jeaffreson, John Cordy (editor): *Middlesex County Records,* III, 264-5; IV, 299-300.

The Devils Cabinet Broke Open (1658) (Guildhall Library), p. 40.

Rebels no Saints (1661) (British Library), pp. 82-3.

The History of the Life of Thomas Ellwood (1714), pp. 191-2.

A Narrative of the Apprehending, Commitment, Arraignment, Condemnation, and Execution of John James (1662) (British Library), p. 26.

Dictionary of National Biography (ref. *John Ketch*).

Marks, Alfred: *Tyburn Tree: Its History and Annals,* pp. 199-201.

The Life and Times of Anthony Wood (edited by Andrew Clark) (1891-5), II, 552-4; III, 177.

Parry, Sir Edward: *The Bloody Assize* (1929), p. 196.

Muddiman, J. G. (editor): *The Bloody Assizes* (1929), p. 29.

Correspondence of the Family of Hatton (1878), II, 32.

Burnet, Gilbert: *History of My Own Time* (Osmund Airy ed., 1900), II, 382-4.

The Apologie of John Ketch Esq. (1683) (British Library).

Echard, Laurence: *The History of England* (1707-18), III, 741, 772-3.

Roberts, George: *The Life, Progresses, and Rebellion of James, Duke of Monmouth* (1844), II, 148-52.

Somers, John: *A Collection of Scarce and Valuable Tracts* (Sir Walter Scott ed., 1809-15), IX, 260-4.

Bramston, Sir John: *Autobiography* (1845), pp. 192-3.

Fraser, Sir William: *The Scotts of Buccleuch* (1878), I, 451-2.

Evelyn, John: *Diary* (E. S. de Beer ed., Clarendon Press, 1955), IV, 456.

The Man of Destiny's hard Fortune (1679) (British Library).

Registers of St James, Clerkenwell, vol V.

Luttrell, Narcissus: *A Brief Historical Relation of State Affairs* (1857), I, 370, 378.

Middlesex County Records: Calendar of Sessions Books (typewritten series), Vols 402-439, January 1682-3 to July 1686, pp. 126-7.

A Pleasant Discourse by way of Dialogue, between the Old and New Jack Catch (1686) (Guildhall Library).

Calendar of State Papers (Domestic Series), James II, II, 48.

Old Bailey Sessions Papers, 20-22 May 1686.

4. SCIONS OF AN ILLUSTRIOUS FAMILY

Edinburgh Town Council Minutes (Edinburgh City Archives), 1 July 1681, 20 August 1684, 30 August 1700, 20 August 1701 and 1 July 1702.

Scott, Sir Walter (editor): *Chronological Notes of Scottish Affairs* (1822), pp. 22, 98-9, 233-6.

Lauder, Sir John: *Historical Notices of Scotish Affairs* (1848), I, 295-6; II, 552.

Lauder, Sir John: *The Decisions of the Lords of Council and Session* (1759-61), I, 169.

Ormiston, Thomas Lane: *The Ormistons of Teviotdale* (1951), pp. 49-50 and pedigree no. 70.

The Register of Interments in the Greyfriars Burying-Ground, Edinburgh, 1658-1700.

The Register of Marriages for the Parish of Edinburgh, 1595-1700.

Carstares, William: *State-Papers and Letters* (1774), pp. 615-16.

Chambers's Edinburgh Journal, 22 February 1834.

Chambers, Robert: *Domestic Annals of Scotland* (1858), II, 461.

Newspapers:
The Post Man, 29 June-2 July 1700.
The Flying Post, 29 June-2 July; 6-8, 13-15, 17-20 and 20-22 August 1700.

5. THE SAILOR, THE BLACKSMITH AND THE BAILIFF'S FOLLOWER

Court of Aldermen: Reports and Papers, 1705-6 (Corporation of London Record Office).
Bleackley, Horace: *The Hangmen of England*, pp. 9-19, 23-35.
A Compleat Collection of Remarkable Tryals...of the most Notorious Malefactors (1721), IV, 240-7.
Smith, Captain Alexander: *The Comical and Tragical History of the Lives and Adventures of the most Noted Bayliffs in and about London and Westminster* (1723), pp. 26-8.
Old Bailey Sessions Papers, 7-9 December 1709, 6-8 December 1710, 23-26 April 1718, 14-16 October 1719.
The History of the Press-yard (1717), pp. 59-62.
Select Trials for Murders, Robberies, Rapes, Sodomy, Coining, Frauds, and other Offences at the Sessions-House in the Old-Bailey (1734-5), I, 55-9.
Howson, Gerald: *Thief-Taker General* (Hutchinson, 1970), p. 107.
Babington, Anthony: *The English Bastille* (Macdonald, 1971), p. 72.
Coldham, Peter Wilson: *English Convicts in Colonial America* (Polyanthos, New Orleans, 1974-6), II, Appendix, p. iii.

Newspapers:
The Weekly-Journal or Saturday's-Post, 9 March 1716; 9 and 30 November and 7 December 1717; 15 March, 26 April and 31 May 1718; 26 September, 17 and 24 October 1719; 28 May 1720.
The Original Weekly Journal, 24-31 August, 2-9, 9-16 and 16-23 November 1717; 7-14 June 1718, 24 October 1719.
The Weekly Journal or British Gazetteer, 7 June 1718.
The St. James's Evening Post, 10-13 March 1716.
The Daily Post, 16 October 1719.

6. 'DICK ARNOLD' AND THE COMICAL FELLOW

Bleackley, Horace: *The Hangmen of England*, pp. 39-67.
Smith, Captain Alexander: *Memoirs of the Life and Times of the famous Jonathan Wild* (1726), pp. 8-9, 19.
A Seasonable Hue and Cry after the Pretender (1719 ed.). *
Marks, Alfred: *Tyburn Tree: Its History and Annals*, pp. 229-36.
Bleackley, Horace (editor): *The Trial of Jack Sheppard* (1933), p. 204.
Howson, Gerald: *Thief-Taker General*, pp. 274-6.
Registers of St Nicholas, Deptford Green (London Metropolitan Archives) .
Select Trials at the Sessions-House in the Old-Bailey (1742), II, 332, 336.
Young, Sidney: *Annals of the Barber-Surgeons* (1890), pp. 417, 421.
The Gentleman's Magazine, 1733, p. 267.

Newspapers:
The Weekly Journal or British Gazetteer (or *Read's Weekly Journal or British Gazetteer*), 18 April 1719; 29 May and 12 June 1725; 4 and 11 May and 17 August 1728; 10 March 1733.
Mist's Weekly Journal, 1 May 1725; 24 August 1728.
The London Journal, 17 August 1728.
The Gloucester Journal, 20 August 1728.
Brice's Weekly Journal, 30 August 1728.
The Country Journal or the Craftsman, 12 June 1731; 10 March and 28 April 1733.
The Universal Spectator and Weekly Journal, 10 and 31 March and 5 May 1733.
The British Journal, 21 February 1730.
The Daily Courant, 11 June 1731.
The Old Whig, 13 March 1735.

7. ANOTHER HANGMAN CONVICTED OF MURDER

Bleackley, Horace: *The Hangmen of England*, pp. 71-89.
Young, Sidney: *Annals of the Barber-Surgeons*, pp. 358, 418, 421.
The Gentleman's Magazine, 1738, p. 659; 1739, p. 46; 1740, p. 570; 1746, pp. 391-4; 1752, pp. 240-1.
Thomson, Mrs Katherine: *Memoirs of the Jacobites* (1845-6), III, 447-8.

* This was advertised in *The Weekly Journal or British Gazetteer* of 21 March 1719.

The Ordinary's Account, 20 December 1738.
Old Bailey Sessions Papers, 29 June-1 July 1743; 25-30 April 1750.
A Journal of the Shrievalty of Richard Hoare, Esquire, in the Years 1740-41 (1815), pp. 37-8, 42-3.

Newspapers:
The Old Whig, 13 March 1735.
The General Evening Post, 22-25 May and 24-27 July 1736.
The Weekly Miscellany, 29 May and 5 June 1736; 23 December 1738; 14 February and 11 April 1741.
The Country Journal or the Craftsman, 29 November 1740.
The London Evening-Post, 18-20 January 1743.
The Daily Gazetteer, 26 January 1741.
Read's Weekly Journal or British Gazetteer, 19 June 1736; 12 and 26 May and 2 June 1750.
Old England, 22 September 1750; 23 May 1752.
The General Advertiser, 25 and 28 September 1750.
The Penny London Post, 3-5 and 15-17 October 1750.
The London Daily Advertiser, 14 May 1752.
The Covent-Garden Journal, 16 May 1752.

8. LAST LONDON HANGMEN OF THE TYBURN ERA

Bleackley, Horace: *The Hangmen of England*, pp. 93-132.
Old Bailey Sessions Papers, 25-30 June 1752; 28 June 1780 and following days.
The Gentleman's Magazine, 1760, pp. 235-6; 1771, p. 141; 1780, p. 343; 1783, p. 990.
Rumbelow, Donald: *The Triple Tree* (Harrap, 1982), pp. 38, 177.
Marks, Alfred: *Tyburn Tree: Its History and Annals*, pp. 249-52.
Mencken, August (editor): *By the Neck* (Hastings House, New York, 1942), pp. 245-51.
Griffiths, Arthur: *The Chronicles of Newgate* (Bracken Books ed., 1987), p. 169.
Pottle, Frederick A. (editor): *Boswell's London Journal* (William Heinemann Ltd., 1950), pp. 251-2.
Repertories of the Court of Aldermen, 1814-15 (Corporation of London Record Office), pp. 510-11.
The Attic Miscellany (1791), I, 166-7.

Newspapers:
The Covent-Garden Journal, 16 May 1752.
Read's Weekly Journal or British-Gazetteer, 16 and 23 May 1752.
The Public Advertiser, 12 April 1771; 14, 22 and 25 July 1780; 11 August 1780.
The London Chronicle, 11-13 April 1771; 15-17 June 1780; 1-4, 6-8 and 13-15 July 1780; 26-28 July 1781.
The Morning Post and Daily Advertiser, 4 July 1780.
The London Courant and Westminster Chronicle, 12 July 1780.
The Daily Universal Register, 22 and 27 November 1786.

9. A DUMFRIES HANGMAN AND HIS DUES

Dumfries Town Council Minutes (Dumfries and Galloway Council Archives), 17 April 1758; 23 December 1760; 23 March 1770; 12 November and 3 December 1781; 14 January and 10 May 1782; 1 and 23 August and 22 September 1785; 16 December 1786; 16 January 1787; 14 and 20 December 1789.
Court of Session Minute Book (printed) (National Archives of Scotland), 9 March and 21 June 1782; 8 February 1783.
Court of Session Process Papers (National Archives of Scotland), ref. *CS29/8 February 1783/Magistrates of Dumfries v Johnston.**
McDowall, William: *History of Dumfries* (1867), pp. 692-5.
Chambers's Edinburgh Journal, 22 February 1834.

Newspapers:
The Edinburgh Evening Courant, 4 July 1772.
The Aberdeen Journal, 8 June 1789.

10. A MISCELLANY

(i) William Sutherland
Wodrow, Robert: *The History of the Sufferings of the Church of Scotland* (1721-2), I, 260 and Appendix no. 11.

* This batch of papers includes the document reproduced on p. 84.

(ii) John Dalgleish
Edinburgh Town Council Minutes, 9 August 1721; 25 July 1722; 28 December 1748; 8 March 1749.
Chambers, Robert: *Domestic Annals of Scotland* (enlarged edition, 1859-61), III, 500-2.
High Court Minute Book (National Archives of Scotland), ref. *JC 7/12*).
Roughead, William (editor): *Trial of Captain Porteous* (1909).
The Gentleman's Magazine, 1746, p. 325.
McLeod Bundle 31A Item 41 (Shelf 131), Edinburgh City Archives.*

Newspapers:
The Caledonian Mercury, 29 March 1742; 18 July 1748.
The Weekly Journal or British Gazetteer, 18 May 1728.
The London Journal, 9 August 1729.

(iii) Andrew Boyle
Edinburgh Town Council Minutes, 1 July 1767; 2 March and 27 July 1768.

Newspapers:
The Caledonian Mercury, 27 February and 14 May 1768.
The Edinburgh Evening Courant, 27 February 1768.

(iv) John Rankine
Stirling Town Council Minutes (Central Regional Council Archives Dept., Stirling), 2 February 1771.
Stirling Burgh Accounts 1789-90 (Central Regional Council Archives Dept., Stirling).

(v) Thomas Woodham
Western Circuit Gaol Book (Public Record Office, ref. *ASSI 23/8 part 2*).
Gloucestershire Notes and Queries, IV, 266-7.

Newspapers:
The London Chronicle, 6-9 August 1785.
The General Evening Post 13-16 August 1785.

(vi) Edward Edwards and John Babington
Court of Great Sessions Minute Book (National Library of Wales), March 1769.

---

* This is the reference for the notice reproduced on p. 90.

Lloyd's Evening Post, 19-21 June 1769.
Calendar of Treasury Books and Papers, 8 June 1743; 9 April 1745.

11. BRUNSKILL AND HIS MATE

Bleackley, Horace: *The Hangmen of England*, pp. 135-61.
Repertories of the Court of Aldermen, 1814-15, pp. 471-3, 510-11; 1816-17, pp. 368-71.
The Gentleman's Magazine, 1797, I, 520; 1807, I, 171.
Radzinowicz, Sir Leon: *A History of the English Criminal Law and its Administration from 1751* (1948-68), I, 147.
Notes and Queries, 1st Series, XII, 293.
Rumbelow, Donald: *The Triple Tree*, p. 188.

Newspapers:
The Daily Universal Register, 27 November 1786.
The Times, 30 January 1794; 23 August 1814.
Bell's Weekly Messenger, 4 May 1817.

12. OLD NED

Hall, Joseph: *Lancaster Castle; its History and Associations* (1843), pp. 49-50, 55-6.
Calendar of Crown Prisoners (Lancashire Record Office), March 1806.
Bishops' Transcripts, St Mary's Church, Lancaster (Lancashire Record Office), December 1812.

Newspapers:
Lancaster Gazette, 22 and 29 March 1806; 12 December 1812.
Cowdroy's Manchester Gazette and Weekly Advertiser, 19 December 1812.
The Morning Post, 11 April 1806.

13. A MAN FROM THE HULKS

York History, No 1, pp. 47-51.

Calendars of Felons, York Assizes (North Yorkshire County Library), 18 March 1793; 13 July 1793; 18 July 1801.
York Assize Records (Public Record Office), refs. *ASSI 44/108, 44/116 and 41/10.*
Knipe, William: *Criminal Chronology of York Castle* (1867), pp. 139, 197, 198.
General Gaol Delivery, York Assizes (North Yorkshire County Library), 18 March 1793; 23 July 1814; 11 March 1815.
Thirsk Burial Register (North Yorkshire County Archives Dept.), 10 March 1841.
Calendar of Prisoners, York Assizes (North Yorkshire County Archives Dept.), 18 July 1835.

Newspapers:
The York Courant, 18 and 25 March 1793; 18 August 1800; 23 March 1801; 17 April 1821; 7 April 1836; 16 April 1840.
The York Herald, 7, 14 and 21 March 1801; 8 September 1821.
The Yorkshire Gazette, 21 April 1821; 8 September 1821; 14 November 1835.
The Times, 24 April 1821.

14. A GUINEA A WEEK OVER THE PRISON GATE

Bleackley, Horace: *The Hangmen of England*, pp. 165-205.
Repertories of the Court of Aldermen, 1814-15, pp. 471-3; 1816-17, pp. 368-9; 1818-19, pp. 19-23; 350-2; 1823-4, p. 393; 1827-8, pp. 535-6; 1829-30, pp. 463-4.
Erredge, John Ackerson: *History of Brighthelmstone* (1862), pp. 335-6.
Curtis, J.: *An Authentic and Faithful History of the Mysterious Murder of Maria Marten* (1828), pp. 301-2.
The Gentleman's Magazine, 1829, I, 282.
Notes and Queries, 2nd Series, XI, 314-16.

Newspapers:
Morning Advertiser, 7 October 1837.
The Times, 2 February 1820; 3 January 1827; 16 February and 20 August 1829; 13 July 1830.
The Morning Chronicle, 2 May 1820.
The Observer, 5 April 1829.
Bell's Life in London, 15 and 22 February and 5 April 1829.

15. NEITHER A SAMSON NOR A HERCULES

Young, Alex F.: *The Encyclopaedia of Scottish Executions, 1750 to 1963* (Eric Dobby Publishing Ltd., 1998), pp. 152-3.
Strathclyde Regional Archives (Glasgow), ref. *A2/1/3*, pp. 59-61.
Pagan, James (editor): *Glasgow, Past and Present* (1851-6), I, 230-2; II, 152-5.
The Gentleman's Magazine, 1820, II, 268-9.
Stirling Council Archive Services, ref. *SB/1/11:BH/24.*

Newspapers:
The Glasgow Herald, 26 March 1856.
The Scots Times (Glasgow), 11 November 1837.
The Times, 17 December 1816; 13 and 20 April and 9 November 1819; 17 May 1825.
Glasgow Courier, 12 September 1820.

16. ANOTHER PLACE, ANOTHER NAME, THE SAME PROFESSION

Edinburgh Town Council Minutes, 3 May 1780; 30 July 1800; 4 January 1809; 5 March 1817.
Chambers's Edinburgh Journal, 22 February 1834.

Newspapers:
Bell's Weekly Messenger, 8 November 1819.
The Times, 17 December 1816; 20 April 1819.
The Edinburgh Evening Courant, 6 March 1817.
Caledonian Mercury, 31 December 1818; 2 January 1819.

17. A SECOND MISCELLANY

(i) Donald Ross
Newton, Norman S.: *The Life and Times of Inverness* (John Donald Publishers Ltd., 1996), pp. 74, 87-9

Newspapers:
Inverness Courier, 25 December 1833.

Inverness Journal, 25 April 1811.

(ii) Hangmen of Aberdeen
Information from the *Town Council Registers* and *Burgh Accounts,* supplied by the Office of the Town Clerk and Chief Executive.
Adams, Norman: *Hangman's Brae* (Tolbooth Books, Banchory, 1993), pp. 12-16.
Correspondence concerning John Milne's appointment published in the *Aberdeen Free Press,* 4 October 1876.

Other Newspapers:
The Aberdeen Journal, 1 July 1788; 15 October 1831.
Caledonian Mercury, 9 November 1818, 11 October 1830.
The Times, 13 October 1830.

(iii) James Aird
Ayr Town Council Minutes (Ayrshire Archives Centre, Ayr), 6 December 1815, 16 August 1823.
Air Advertiser, 14 August 1823.

(iv) Samuel Burrows
Jones, Lewis: *Jones' Handbook for Ruthin and Vicinity* (1884), pp. 20-1.

Newspapers:
The Lancaster Gazette, 19 October 1816.
Chester Courant and Anglo-Welsh Gazette, 21 September 1830.

(v) John Williams
Edinburgh Town Council Minutes, 27 March 1833; 28 July 1835.

Newspapers:
The Times, 8 October 1833.
The Edinburgh Evening Courant, 16 July 1835.

18. A HANGMAN KILLED BY AN ALCOHOLIC

Edinburgh Town Council Minutes, 28 July 1835, 24 August 1847.
Records of the High Court of Justiciary (National Archives of Scotland), refs. *JC8/54, JC4/51 no. 50* and *AD14/47/565.*

Newspapers:
The Edinburgh Evening Courant, 6 August 1835.
The Times, 8 August 1835, 8 April 1844.
Caledonian Mercury, 19 October 1837, 18 April 1840, 16 and 26 August 1847.

19. A HANGMAN AGED EIGHTY-FOUR

The Life and Recollections of Calcraft the Hangman (1880), p. 239.

Newspapers:
The Glasgow Herald, 1 February 1850, 26 March 1856.
The Times, 19 May 1841, 8 April 1844, 29 October 1849, 20 August 1850, 28 October 1851.
Stirling Journal, 6 October 1843.

20. A HANGMAN FOR FORTY-FIVE YEARS

Bleackley, Horace: *The Hangmen of England*, pp. 209-27, 231-46.
Family Tree Magazine, September 1995, pp. 3-5.
Griffiths, Arthur: *The Chronicles of Newgate*, pp. 441, 523-6.
Cooper, David D.: *The Lesson of the Scaffold* (Allen Lane, 1974), pp. 15-20, 22-3, 73.
Borowitz, Albert: *The Bermondsey Horror* (Robson Books, 1989), p. 254.
Fielding, Steve: *The Hangman's Record* (Chancery House Press, 1994-), I, 1-36, 44-5, 286.
The Life and Recollections of Calcraft the Hangman (1880), pp. 95, 240.
Quarterly Indexes of Deaths, England and Wales (Family Records Centre), June 1855 (Sarah Calcraft), December 1870 (Louisa Calcraft).
Ms 12357E (National Library of Wales), pp. 1353, 1358.
Papers of Griffith E. Owen (National Library of Wales).

Newspapers:
The Observer, 5 April 1829.
Bell's Life in London, 5 April 1829, 19 December 1830.
The Times, 14 April 1829; 25 February 1846; 14 and 19 November 1849; 7 and 14 March and 15 April 1850; 1 and 2 April 1856; 10 January 1861; 13 January 1874; 21 December 1875; 17 December 1879.

The Carnarvon and Denbigh Herald, 5 April 1862.
Pall Mall Gazette, 21 and 23 October 1869.
Western Mail (Cardiff), 28 August 1901.
The Daily Telegraph, 17 December 1879.
The Morning Advertiser, 16 December, 1879.
The Illustrated Police News, 27 December 1879.

21. THE LAST YORK HANGMEN

Knipe, William: *Criminal Chronology of York Castle*, pp. 198-243, 248.
Fielding, Steve: *The Hangman's Record*, I, 80, 286.

Newspapers:
The York Courant, 16 April 1840.
The York Herald, 16 April 1853, 14 December 1878 (two separate items).
The Times, 28 August 1850; 10 January and 12 August 1859; 2 January and 28 December 1860; 24 December 1862; 22 June, 11 August and 12 September 1864; 17 March 1865; 13 May and 29 December 1868; 22 December 1875; 4 April 1877.

22. SMITH OF DUDLEY

Tump, Aristotle: *Black Country Characters* (Bugle Publications, 1986), pp. 8-33.
Knott, George H.: *Trial of William Palmer* (1912), p. 348.
Fielding, Steve: *The Hangman's Record*, I, 2-3, 29-31, 291.

Newspapers:
The Derby and Derbyshire Gazette, 10 April 1874.
The Staffordshire Advertiser, 18 April 1840, 21 June 1856, 15 August 1857, 17 August 1872.
The Times, 16 June 1856, 13 January 1866, 8 August 1866.
The Derby Mercury, 18 June 1856.
The Chester Chronicle and Cheshire and North Wales Advertiser, 30 April 1841.
The Warwick and Warwickshire Advertiser, 25 August 1860.

The Warwick and Leamington Times, 11 January 1873.
Express and Star (Wolverhampton), 16 July 1968.

CONCLUSION

The Law Journal, 28 August 1926, pp. 150-1.
Bailey, Brian: *Hangmen of England* (W. H. Allen, 1989), pp. 108, 140, 192.
Scott, George Ryley: *The History of Capital Punishment* (1950), p. 141.
Bleackley, Horace: *The Hangmen of England*, pp. 233-4.
Pierrepoint, Albert: *Executioner: Pierrepoint* (Coronet ed., 1977), pp. 27, 34, 36, 37.
Dernley, Syd, with Newman, David: *The Hangman's Tale* (Pan ed., 1990), p. 200.

Index